Editor
Erica N. Russikoff, M.A.

Illustrator
Clint McKnight

Editor in Chief
Karen J. Goldfluss, M.S. Ed.

Cover Artist
Brenda DiAntonis

Art Coordinator
Renée Mc Elwee

Imaging
Leonard P. Swierski

Publisher
Mary D. Smith, M.S. Ed.

Spotlight On
AMERICA

Grades 5–8

A Nation of Immigrants

Author
Robert W. Smith

Teacher Created Resources
6421 Industry Way
Westminster, CA 92683
www.teachercreated.com

ISBN: 978-1-4206-31

© 2011 Teacher Created Re
Made in U.S.A.

D1319496

Teacher Created Resources

Table of Contents

| 1600 | 1650 | 1700 | 1750 | 1800 | 1850 | 1900 | 1950 | 2000 |

Introduction

The *Spotlight on America* series is designed to introduce some of the seminal events in American history to students in the fifth through eighth grades. Reading in the content area is enriched with a balanced variety of activities in written language, literature, social studies, and oral expression. The series is designed to make history literally come alive in your classroom and take root in the minds of your students.

A Nation of Immigrants

The entire history of the United States is inextricably linked with immigration because the United States is a nation of immigrants. Even the approximately ten million American Indians, who lived in the area later to become the United States, were the descendants of immigrants who migrated across the Bering Sea from Asia over the course of 30,000 years. The early English colonies were populated primarily by immigrants from the British Isles and Northern Europe in the first two centuries of settlement. Later, more waves of immigration came from these same sources through the 1860s. The California Gold Rush brought immigrants from Asia, as well as Europe. The four decades from the 1880s to the 1920s brought masses of people from Southern and Eastern Europe. The last sixty years have seen immigrants coming from all over the world, but especially from Latin American and Asian nations.

Reading Comprehension

The reading selections and comprehension questions in this book serve to introduce some of the trends in American immigration, as well as some of the interesting people and cultures who have enriched the nation with their energy, drive, and character. People from many nations and ethnicities have blended to create a distinctly American culture woven from the contributions of Europe, Asia, Africa, and Latin America. Students will be able to find the threads of their own roots in their reading about the many peoples who populated the nation.

Activities

The reading selections in this book set the stage for activities in other subject areas. The literature selections are intended to bring students into the lives of these immigrants. The activities in written language, biography, and research are designed to help students recognize and empathize with the lives of immigrants. The activities with timelines, maps, and other social studies projects provide students with a sense of time, place, and historical perspective. The culminating activities aim to give students a sense of living history. Enjoy using this book with your students, and look for other books in this series.

Teacher Lesson Plans for Reading Comprehension

The First Wave (1600–1775)

Objective: Students will demonstrate fluency and comprehension in reading historically based text.

Materials: copies of The First Wave (1600–1775) (pages 7–9) and The First Wave (1600–1775) Quiz (page 34); additional reading selections from books, encyclopedias, and Internet sources for enrichment

Procedure

1. Reproduce and distribute The First Wave (1600–1775) reading selection listed above. Review pre-reading skills by briefly reviewing text and encouraging students to underline, make notes in the margins, write questions, and highlight unfamiliar words as they read.

2. Have students read the selection independently, in small groups, or together as a class.

3. As a class, discuss the following questions (or others of your choosing):

   • Would you have come to America in the colonial period? What would be the advantages and disadvantages?

   • What do you think was the most important motive for coming to America in the colonial period? Explain.

   • Why do you think people fought over religious beliefs?

Assessment: Have students complete The First Wave (1600–1775) Quiz and underline the sentences in the reading selection where the answers were found. Correct the quiz together.

The Second Wave (1820–1870)

Objective: Students will demonstrate fluency and comprehension in reading historically based text.

Materials: copies of The Second Wave (1820–1870) (pages 10–13) and The Second Wave (1820–1870) Quiz (page 35); additional reading selections from books, encyclopedias, and Internet sources for enrichment

Procedure

1. Reproduce and distribute The Second Wave (1820–1870) reading selection listed above. Review pre-reading skills by briefly reviewing text and encouraging students to underline, make notes in the margins, write questions, and highlight unfamiliar words as they read.

2. Have students read the selection independently, in small groups, or together as a class.

3. As a class, discuss the following questions (or others of your choosing):

   • Which immigrant group do you think was the most desperate to immigrate to America? Why do you think so?

   • Which group would you have liked to immigrate with? Explain your choice.

   • Why did Americans resent immigrants? Did they have any good reasons for this resentment?

Assessment: Have students complete The Second Wave (1820–1870) Quiz and underline the sentences in the reading selection where the answers were found. Correct the quiz together.

Teacher Lesson Plans
for Reading Comprehension *(cont.)*

The Third Wave (1880–1920)

Objective: Students will demonstrate fluency and comprehension in reading historically based text.

Materials: copies of The Third Wave (1880–1920) (pages 14–16) and The Third Wave (1880–1920) Quiz (page 36); additional reading selections from books, encyclopedias, and Internet sources for enrichment

Procedure

1. Reproduce and distribute The Third Wave (1880–1920) reading selection listed above. Review pre-reading skills by briefly reviewing text and encouraging students to underline, make notes in the margins, write questions, and highlight unfamiliar words as they read.

2. Have students read the selection independently, in small groups, or together as a class.

3. As a class, discuss the following questions (or others of your choosing):

   • What was the difference between the "old immigrants" and the "new immigrants"?

   • How would you feel if you were an immigrant child who had to work and was unable to attend school or play?

   • Should the United States place quotas on the number of immigrants from one nation or culture? Why?

Assessment: Have students complete The Third Wave (1880–1920) Quiz and underline the sentences in the reading selection where the answers were found. Correct the quiz together.

Ellis Island: Gateway to America

Objective: Students will demonstrate fluency and comprehension in reading historically based text.

Materials: copies of Ellis Island: Gateway to America (pages 17–21) and Ellis Island: Gateway to America Quiz (page 37); additional reading selections from books, encyclopedias, and Internet sources for enrichment

Procedure

1. Reproduce and distribute Ellis Island: Gateway to America reading selection listed above. Review pre-reading skills by briefly reviewing text and encouraging students to underline, make notes in the margins, write questions, and highlight unfamiliar words as they read.

2. Have students read the selection independently, in small groups, or together as a class.

3. As a class, discuss the following questions (or others of your choosing):

   • What good things did the officials at Ellis Island do?

   • Were the restrictions and examinations imposed at Ellis Island necessary and fair? Explain your reasons.

   • How do you think women felt about being mail-order brides?

Assessment: Have students complete the Ellis Island: Gateway to America Quiz and underline the sentences in the reading selection where the answers were found. Correct the quiz together.

Teacher Lesson Plans
for Reading Comprehension *(cont.)*

Angel Island and The Fourth Wave (1945–Present)

Objective: Students will demonstrate fluency and comprehension in reading historically based text.

Materials: copies of Angel Island (pages 22–25) and The Fourth Wave (1945–Present) (pages 26–27) and quizzes (pages 38 and 39); additional reading selections from books, encyclopedias, and Internet sources for enrichment

Procedure

1. Reproduce and distribute Angel Island and The Fourth Wave (1945–Present) reading selections listed above on separate days. Review pre-reading skills by briefly reviewing text and encouraging students to underline, make notes in the margins, write questions, and highlight unfamiliar words as they read.

2. Have students read each selection independently, in small groups, or together as a class.

3. As a class, discuss the following questions (or others of your choosing):

    • Compare the treatment of immigrants at Angel Island and Ellis Island. Why was the treatment different?

    • Why do immigrants come to America today?

    • How are immigrants treated in America today compared to earlier groups of immigrants?

Assessment: Have students complete each quiz (Angel Island and The Fourth Wave) and underline the sentences in the reading selections where the answers were found. Correct the quizzes together.

Famous Immigrants, Parts I and II

Objective: Students will demonstrate fluency and comprehension in reading historically based text.

Materials: copies of Famous Immigrants, Parts I and II (pages 28–30 and 31–33) and quizzes (pages 40 and 41); additional reading selections from books, encyclopedias, and Internet sources for enrichment

Procedure

1. Reproduce and distribute Famous Immigrants, Parts I and II reading selections listed above. Review pre-reading skills by briefly reviewing text and encouraging students to underline, make notes in the margins, write questions, and highlight unfamiliar words as they read.

2. Have students read the selections independently, in small groups, or together as a class.

3. As a class, discuss the following questions (or others of your choosing):

    • Which famous immigrant did you most admire? Why?

    • Which famous immigrant did you dislike? Why?

    • Which immigrant was the most important to America? Why?

    • Which immigrant would you have liked to talk to or learn from? Why?

Assessment: Have students complete the Famous Immigrant, Parts I and II quizzes and underline the sentences in the reading selections where the answers were found. Correct the quizzes together.

Reading
Passages

The First Wave (1600–1775)

The First Americans

The first immigrants to arrive in the area that is now the United States came across a land bridge between Asia and North America thousands of years ago. Like people throughout history, they migrated across the earth. These migrants followed the animals they were hunting and arrived in the central part of North America several thousand years ago. They spread across the continent in tribes of mostly related peoples. These American Indians, while originally immigrants themselves, had well-established communities where they lived, hunted, fought with other tribes, and usually prospered. There were probably about ten million American Indians living in the area now called the United States during the early colonial period.

European Exploration Starts a Migration

The discoveries of Christopher Columbus and the voyages of English, French, and Spanish explorers led first to small settlements in New England and Virginia by the British and in Florida by the Spanish. French explorers traveled along the northern edge of what is now the United States and down the Mississippi and its tributaries. Some Spanish colonists settled in Florida, and a few French colonists settled in what is now Canada.

The First Wave

The area that is now the United States experienced a wave of immigration, which arrived in surges from the early 1600s to the beginning of the Revolutionary War in 1775. Most of the earliest immigrants were English, but many other settlers came from Ireland, Wales, and Scotland in the British Isles. Colonists also came from France, the Netherlands, and Germany.

Economic Motivation

These early immigrants were motivated to leave the safety of home, travel on a long and dangerous ocean journey, and face the unknown dangers of the New World for a variety of economic reasons. Some early colonial settlers came for adventure or the hope of finding quick and easy wealth in the New World, as some of the early settlers at Jamestown did. However, most immigrants to America in this period were young, poor, male, single, and had little or no education either in school or in learning a trade. Many of the early English immigrants were hoping to own large tracts of land or start their own businesses.

Reading Passages

The First Wave (1600–1775) *(cont.)*

Indentured Servants

Economic survival was the main motivation for most immigrants. Some were so poor in their native countries that they sold themselves and their families as indentured servants to acquire enough money for sea passage to the colonies. They were then required to work seven years (or longer) under slave conditions for the people who bought their contracts. About 300,000 European immigrants from 1607 to 1789 were indentured servants.

Convicts and Debtors

Because English jails were overflowing with criminals arrested for minor crimes, officials sometimes reduced the overcrowding by sending convicts to the New World. This was especially true for debtors. Men who owed money for debts they could not pay were imprisoned, sometimes with their entire families, until they could pay off the debt. They couldn't work at a job in jail, so many prisons were filled with people whose only crime was owing money. Many of these debtors and their families were sent to the colonies. In fact, the colony of Georgia was founded as a refuge for debtors. Approximately 50,000 immigrants during the colonial period were convicts or debtors.

Religious and Political Persecution

Religious persecution by the authorities was another reason for immigrating. The Puritans and other religious groups who settled in Massachusetts and Connecticut were escaping harsh laws and religious restrictions in England. Catholic colonists in Maryland and Quakers in Pennsylvania settled in these colonies because the proprietors (founders) of the colonies were given land by the king as a way of letting these unpopular religious groups leave England, where they were often victims of persecution by the authorities.

Involuntary Immigrants: African Slaves

The first few Africans arrived in the British colony of Jamestown as indentured servants, but soon they arrived in large shiploads to be sold as slaves. Africans were sold in the southern colonies to work on plantations and in the northern colonies for work on farms and in households. The continual purchase of new slaves from Africa led to over 350,000 unwilling immigrants. Slave life was degrading and physically exhausting, and many slaves died young from overwork and abuse. It became illegal to purchase slaves from Africa after 1808 in the United States.

The First Wave (1600–1775) *(cont.)*

New Arrivals

The 250,000 settlers in the American colonies in 1700 were joined by more than 400,000 immigrants by the start of the Revolutionary War in 1775. Many more immigrants came from Ireland, Germany, and Scotland for the same reasons as the earlier immigrants, especially religious and political persecution and financial distress. Economic motivation was the primary cause for immigration from other countries. In the colonial period, at least 100,000 Irish immigrants arrived in America. They came with the hope of escaping poverty and finding better paying jobs or land to farm. They settled in many colonies and often succeeded in owning farms and even plantations in the South. The German immigrants were mostly Protestant and settled in the colony of Pennsylvania.

The Revolutionary War years witnessed less immigration because of the unsettled financial situation and the disruptions of war. However, some immigrants fled English rule in Ireland and some French citizens fled from the French Revolution in the 1790s.

Coming to America

Early immigrants to America faced enormous difficulties in getting to the New World. There were no regularly scheduled trips to the colonies. Immigrants who wanted to cross the ocean had to either wait until a ship was going and pay for the passage or form a group, find a captain with a ship, and arrange passage on his terms. The least expensive fares were still very costly.

The ships were only 40 to 80 feet long, often barely seaworthy, and extremely uncomfortable. The voyage took eight to twelve weeks to cross the Atlantic Ocean. Because they were wind-driven ships, their speeds could vary a great deal,

and some days the ships simply floated while waiting for wind. Most passengers rode below decks and were cold and uncomfortable. Passengers got sick with fevers, scurvy (a disease of the teeth and mouth caused by a lack of vitamins), and dysentery (which caused great distress in the stomach and digestive tract). Seasickness was very common, and there were few opportunities to clean up. Lice, insects, and rats were standard. Children, the elderly, and less healthy adults were most likely to get seriously ill or die.

Reading Passages

The Second Wave (1820–1870)

European Immigrants

Nearly 7.5 million immigrants came to the United States between 1820 and 1870. Most of these new residents came from Europe. About 2.5 million, one-third of the immigrants, were poor people from Ireland. Most of them were trying to escape a severe famine in Ireland that left millions of its citizens starving or dead. These immigrants from Ireland were totally impoverished and usually settled in whatever city they arrived in and tried to get work at any wage they could.

German Immigrants Want Land

Another 2.5 million people were Germans who came to America seeking a better life and, especially, cheap land for farming. They were sometimes able to afford the voyage across the ocean and the railroad fare to the West where they intended to buy cheap land from states, the federal government, or the railroad companies, which had been given huge amounts of land as payment for building the railroads.

HANNIBAL RAILROAD COMPANY
—— Has Received ——
600,000 ACRES OF
FARMING & WOOD LANDS
FOR SALE
In Lots to Suit Purchasers in
NORTHERN MISSOURI
Hannibal, MO

Other Immigrants and Sojourners

Chinese immigrants came to find gold in California and to work on the railroads or in mining. French Canadians moved across the Canadian border to find work in the New England states.

Some foreigners, especially those from Asia, came only to find wealth or work and intended to return to their native lands once they had succeeded. They were called *sojourners*, which means *travelers*.

The Irish Potato Famine

Sir Walter Raleigh introduced the potato, a plant native to Peru, to Ireland when he was given large land grants there in the late 1500s by Queen Elizabeth. It became the basic food grown, especially by poor tenant farmers. In 1845, virtually the entire potato crop in Ireland was destroyed by a blight that turned the potato black, stinking, and inedible. Thousands died and millions suffered from starvation in 1845. The blight returned the next year in even worse form, and the British authorities who ruled Ireland and controlled most of the land were unwilling to help. More than a million Irish died from starvation and more than a million immigrated to the United States during the years of famine in search of work. They hoped to find better economic opportunities and to avoid religious persecution in Ireland from the ruling Protestant authorities in England.

 Reading Passages

The Second Wave (1820–1870) *(cont.)*

Anti-Immigrant Anger

The seemingly endless stream of new arrivals to the United States eventually created a protest movement against immigrants. Wealthy manufacturers liked having a source of cheap labor, but American workers believed correctly that the wave of immigrants kept wages depressed and made organizing unions very difficult. The Know-Nothing Party in the 1850s arose as a reaction to immigrants and Roman Catholics who were predominant among the new immigrants. So many Irish had immigrated to the U.S. that they often encountered hostility and signs in businesses reading, "No Irish need apply."

HELP WANTED
NO IRISH NEED APPLY

Ports of Entry

Philadelphia had been the major port of entry for most immigrants in the first two centuries of the nation's history. Castle Garden, the nation's first immigration station, opened in New York in 1855—just before the Civil War. Many immigrants came to California in the late 1840s during the California Gold Rush. Immigrants from all over the world, including China, were lured by the hope for finding gold. Most entered near San Francisco because it was near the goldfields.

New York City

Between 1820 and 1839, nearly 500,000 immigrants entered through the port of New York. Between 1839 and 1860, another 4.5 million immigrants entered primarily through New York. In the 1840s, about forty passenger ships a day arrived in Manhattan carrying as many as a thousand poverty-stricken immigrants in steerage. Most of the European immigrants who arrived between 1840 and 1850 were poor and settled in New York City. The city had 200,000 residents in 1830. By 1860, it had over a million residents, and over half of them were immigrants. The Irish and other extremely poor immigrants tended to settle into the first city where they arrived. By the 1850s, the working class in New York City would be three-fourths immigrants.

Reading Passages

The Second Wave (1820–1870) *(cont.)*

Steerage Passengers

The immigrants arriving in New York City came out of ships where they had suffered terribly during the voyage across the Atlantic Ocean. With luck, these ships might take five weeks to reach port, but they could take months, and the passengers were in desperate straits. They often suffered from contagious diseases contracted from close contact with as many as a thousand other people cramped below decks in steerage compartments, which provided rotten food; clothing and bedding covered with lice, housing mice, rats, and roaches; and little opportunity for personal hygiene. Once ships unloaded, many immigrants were taken advantage of by con men who cheated them by promising jobs and housing for a fee and then vanishing with the cash.

Castle Garden

Reformers and concerned political leaders convinced the New York State Legislature to systematically help the immigrants and organize the immigration process in the city. In 1855, Castle Garden, an old fort on a tiny island at the foot of Manhattan Island, became the nation's first official immigrant reception center. It was run by the state and reduced the abuse of immigrants by thieves and con men. Ships were inspected on arrival, especially for disease, and emergency medical aid was offered to the ill and the utterly destitute (people with no money or valuables). Food, clothing, and shelter were arranged for the destitute, as well.

Clerks steered passengers traveling to other parts of the country to legitimate railroad and steamship companies. A labor official helped workers find jobs with construction companies,

farms, mines, factories, businesses, and in private homes. Medical officials checked passengers for serious illnesses and quarantined those who were contagious.

West to Farm

Many Germans and other immigrants with money had been lured to America by the promise of cheap land for farming. They often headed to the Midwest, where cheap land was available from railroads and the federal government under the Homestead Act. The Act granted 160 acres to a family if they lived on the land and farmed it for five years. Germans also settled in Midwestern cities, such as Milwaukee, Chicago, Cincinnati, and St. Louis.

 Reading Passages

The Second Wave (1820–1870) *(cont.)*

Asian Immigrants

The Chinese were the first major group of Asian people to immigrate to the United States. The discovery of gold in California encouraged 25,000 Chinese to immigrate to California between 1848 and 1851. Another 30,000 worked as laborers or in service businesses, such as laundries, in other Western states. More than 28,000 Japanese immigrated to Hawaii in the ten years between 1885 and 1895 to work in the sugar industry, and another 26,000 Japanese were hired to work on sugar plantations by 1899.

Building the Transcontinental Railroad

One of the major employers of Chinese laborers in the 1860s was the Central Pacific Railroad. With many Californian men away fighting during the Civil War and others still seeking gold, the owners of the Central Pacific Railroad were desperate for manpower and decided to hire fifty Chinese laborers on a trial basis. The owners were afraid that the relatively small build of the Chinese men would be a liability on the backbreaking work of digging and grading the land for laying track. However, the Chinese had already earned a good reputation as workers in the community. They were soon so valued that the railroad hired all they could find and requested more men from China.

In digging a tunnel through a solid rock mountain, the Chinese were tested against professional miners from other countries and outperformed them at every week's measurement. Ten thousand men built the Central Pacific Railroad. Nine thousand of them were Chinese laborers.

Working Too Hard

Although they were sometimes accused of being slaves by their white counterparts, most Chinese laborers, especially on the railroads, made about the same pay as other workers. Chinese laborers needed fewer overseers and worked longer hours than some other laborers. This led to complaints against them and a desire to exclude them, just as the Irish were unintentionally creating political opposition in the eastern United States.

The Chinese also held some jobs, such as farm workers, domestic servants, and laundrymen, which white workers would not do. The Chinese work ethic was so strong that it sometimes hurt their image in the community.

Reading Passages

The Third Wave (1880–1920)

Old Immigrants, New Immigrants

In the forty years from 1880 to 1920, a deluge of immigrants flooded into the United States in search of work and opportunity.

Previous immigrants, often called "old immigrants," came from northern and western Europe—from Germany, the British Isles, and similar nations. The "new immigrants" came largely from southern and eastern Europe. The new immigrants were fleeing economic, political, and religious persecution in Europe. Jews from Poland and Russia, Catholics from Italy, and the oppressed of many nations in the world arrived. In all, more than twenty-three million people arrived in America during this time.

Incredible Cities

The new immigrants of the late 1800s and early 1900s found an America that they had never imagined. The cities were particularly exciting because they were filled with people, including tens of thousands of immigrants in many cities and hundreds of thousands in New York City. They saw huge bridges spanning bays and rivers, some of them still under construction. Parts of the cities had large department stores and specialty shops with every imaginable product. Horse-drawn carriages, trolleys, and the first automobiles filled the streets with noise and people on the move. The sidewalks were often crowded with people going about their business. The rise of skyscrapers, especially in New York, made it seem as if the newcomers had indeed entered another world.

Immigrant Lifestyles

Most immigrants living in cities were poor and had arrived destitute from Russia, Poland, Austria, Hungary, the Baltic countries, Italy, and other regions of southern and eastern Europe, as well as from Ireland, Germany, and other western European countries. Most immigrants didn't speak English, although most learned it as fast as they were able, especially the terms related to their jobs and family needs. Many immigrant children took advantage of the free public education available in most communities and learned English. Children often became the translators for their families, especially for dealing with government agencies, doctors, and many business entities, such as landlords. Some adults also took night classes in English after working all day, in the hope that they could get better jobs if they knew English.

Reading Passages

The Third Wave (1880–1920) *(cont.)*

Tenement Life

Poor immigrants lived in tenements, which were dingy, dark, dirty buildings six or seven stories high. The landlords built them to make as much money as possible off the immigrants. Families were squeezed into tiny one- or two-room apartments with little light, limited bathrooms, small cooking stoves, and no fresh air. One of these small apartments might house ten or more members of a family. There were as many as thirty-two families, with more than 150 people sometimes, living in each of these buildings. The tenements were stacked so close that 4,000 people might be living on a single block of tenements. Fires were common, and many people, especially the elderly and children, were killed in the rapidly spreading blazes.

Earning a Living

Sometimes, there were lots of jobs, but for the poor and largely uneducated immigrants, the work involved very long hours, poor pay, and back-breaking work. Some men found work as manual laborers on construction jobs, and men and women sometimes were able to find low-paying factory work. Women were often hired for textile work, which required careful work with cloth in making clothes. Young women with educations found that there was work in offices, telephone companies, and retail stores.

There were few unions, with most of them barely surviving, although the effort to organize American unions started during this period. Factory owners would increase workloads, cut pay, and lock workers in the factories during the shifts. There were very few rules enforced by the government to protect workers.

Working Children

Many immigrant children worked in textile factories for a few cents a day. In mining communities, young boys were hired in coal mines to separate coal from rocks on a moving conveyor belt that often cost the children their fingers and sometimes their lives. Children as young as five worked by shelling clams and picking fruit and vegetables in more rural communities.

The cities sometimes provided illegal work for children, as well as opportunities to sell newspapers and articles out of small pushcarts. Some children joined gangs and turned to small-time crime, but most of the immigrant children avoided the gangs. They went to school if they didn't have to work to support their families and got better jobs when they grew up.

Reading Passages

The Third Wave (1880–1920) *(cont.)*

The Streets

The streets became the meeting places for the poor. They met friends and other people who spoke their native languages, practiced their religions, and celebrated their ethnic holidays. Rumors and news quickly passed along, and the street became a center of social life as immigrants climbed the long ladder to success. A few immigrants were successful in the first generation, but many more families succeeded as the children grew up and entered the work force and their children became successes in business, school, and industry.

Immigration Restrictions

The first restrictions on immigration were imposed, which prevented convicts from legally entering the country. New regulations made it difficult for new immigrants to become citizens. California residents blamed the Chinese immigrants for low wages and fewer jobs. California citizens led a fight to exclude new Chinese immigration, which resulted in the Chinese Exclusion Act of 1882.

Controlling Immigration

Anger at the immigrants focused on special groups, although immigrants were blamed in general for low wages and poor working conditions. Anti-immigrant feelings were fanned, especially against Jews, Catholics, and the Japanese, as well as Asians in general. U.S. society already divided by class and race became more fractured. Laws were passed prohibiting beggars, contract laborers, the mentally ill, children without parents, and nearly all Asians from entering the country.

Quotas

In 1921, quotas were placed on immigration from any one country. Most of the acceptable immigrants were from Britain, Germany, and Ireland. Immigration from much of southern and eastern Europe was restricted. There was considerable prejudice against Jews and Catholics from these nations and a fear of the political dangers caused by communism, which had already taken control of some European countries.

Reading
Passages

Ellis Island:
Gateway to America

The Land

Ellis Island was the gateway to America for twelve million immigrants who entered the United States between 1892 and 1924. Located near the Statue of Liberty, the immigration center became the door into the country through which millions of successful immigrants walked. Ellis Island was also the Island of Tears for those people who were excluded from entry into America because they were considered undesirable. Originally named for a New York merchant who bought the three-acre island in the late 1700s, Ellis Island was first purchased by the state of New York and later by the federal government in 1808.

First Federal Immigration Center

The first federal immigration center was opened on Ellis Island on January 1, 1892. The site was expanded to $27\frac{1}{2}$ acres in size and eventually held more than thirty-five buildings. This included the famous Main Building with a Great Hall where more than 5,000 people were processed for entry into America every day during some years of peak immigration. The center was especially busy in the first twenty-five years of its existence. It had long periods of limited use after that and was closed in 1954. After falling into decay, many buildings were refurbished. The center was opened as a part of the Statue of Liberty National Monument in 1965.

Beginnings

The original island had only three acres. It was doubled in size to make room for a large, wooden, two-story immigration center about 400 feet long and 150 feet wide that looked like a seaside hotel of the period. The small six-acre island was expanded with landfill to over twenty-seven acres covered with many additional buildings, a seawall, and docks.

The center opened on January 1, 1892. The huge two-story main building had places for baggage on the first floor and examining rooms on the second floor. There were money exchange centers, railroad ticket counters, snack bars, and offices on the second floor, as well. A few wealthier immigrants who had traveled first or second class by ship were quickly whisked through processing and went on their way into America. The vast majority of immigrants were poor, had traveled in the belly of the passenger ships in steerage, and awaited careful scrutiny at the center.

Reading Passages

Ellis Island:
Gateway to America *(cont.)*

Disastrous Fire

There were many wooden buildings, including a hospital, a laundry, a bathhouse, rooms for doctors and nurses, a dormitory for immigrants who stayed overnight, a power plant, and a dining hall. These buildings were finally completed on June 14, 1897. Incredibly, the entire facility (including all of the new wooden buildings) burned down the next night on June 15, 1897. The facility was completely destroyed as were the immigration records of all the people entering since 1892 at Ellis Island and the immigration records from Castle Island since 1855. Immigrants had entered Ellis Island in the first five years at the rate of over half a million people a year. Millions of immigrants were never able to prove their legal entry into the United States because of the lost records. The cause of the fire was never discovered.

Starting Over

For the next three years, the newly arrived immigrants were processed from a temporary depot at the Battery's Barge office while Ellis Island was rebuilt. A huge new brick building and other rebuilt buildings were opened in December 1900, but the center was hopelessly inadequate even at its opening. The center sometimes had to handle as many as 7,000 immigrants a day. Many immigrants had to wait for days on the ships that brought them before they could be ferried to the processing center.

The Processing

The United States had passed a number of laws in the early 1890s to exclude immigrants who were considered undesirable. Sometimes, it included entire nations and cultures, such as the Chinese and other Asians. Other exclusions were based on the worry that some immigrants

would become criminals, wards of the state unable to earn a living, or people living on the streets.

Looking for Undesirables

Colored chalk was used to mark the clothes of those who needed to be carefully inspected. The inspectors quickly marked for special attention those who had trouble breathing, appeared to have difficulties seeing, the mentally unfit, and anyone with crippled arms or legs or other apparent disabilities. An "X" was used to mark those who might have mental disorders. The letter "K" signified a hernia, "SC" stood for scalp disease, and "H" represented a heart defect.

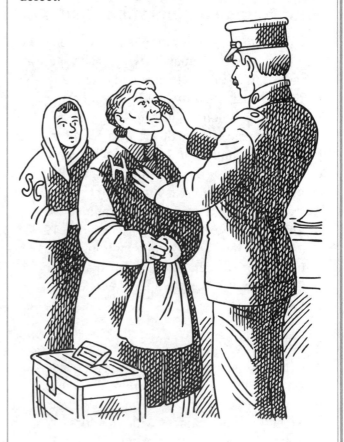

Reading
Passages

Ellis Island:
Gateway to America *(cont.)*

Trachoma Inspections

Some individuals were quarantined immediately in the hospital or sometimes even in a cage. Immigrants with suspected eye infections, especially the feared contagious disease trachoma, were kept apart and carefully checked. A much dreaded, painful eye hook was used to pry up the eye lid and check for signs of this disease. People who had confirmed cases were shipped back to their native countries, as were other individuals who didn't qualify for entrance into the country.

Mentally Handicapped and Silent Children

Those who were deaf and dumb were considered mentally unfit for entry, as well as immigrants who showed any signs of mental illness. Deaf-mute children were sometimes sent back alone because the rest of a family would be allowed to enter, but the disabled child was considered unacceptable. Most immigrants did not speak English, and quiet, fearful children or teens who were silent were carefully checked to see if they could talk and understand. Simple puzzles and tests were sometimes administered to immigrants to make sure they could talk and understand in some language. Many immigrants spoke languages that were unknown to the Ellis Island staff.

Contagious Diseases and Physical Disabilities

Even before they got off the ships, passengers in the steerage section were checked for lice, typhoid fever, smallpox, and other contagious diseases much feared for their capacity to create epidemics. All passengers with physical disabilities had to prove they could function and would be able to work.

Making It Out

Immigrants also had to pass physical and oral exams. Some were simply informational like the immigrant's name and marriage status. Others were designed to trick unwary immigrants. "How will you earn a living?" seemed simple, but you couldn't admit you had a job lined up. It was illegal for some employers or immigrants to arrange jobs before entering the country.

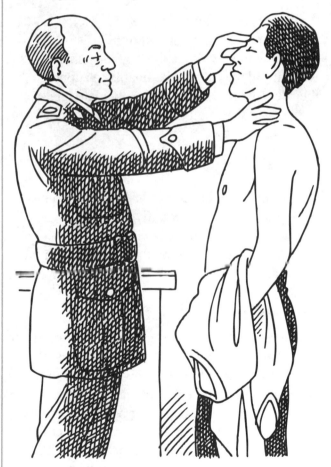

Reading Passages

Ellis Island:
Gateway to America *(cont.)*

Passing the Test and the Bucks

"Do you have any money?" was often tricky, too. Many immigrants were absolutely destitute, having used all their money to pay for their passage or food. Since having $20 or $25 seemed to be enough, immigrants often showed that amount to the inspector and then surreptitiously palmed the money off to other needy people. Sometimes, the same $25 was passed through many families.

"Is someone meeting you?" was especially important for women or children. Even though women worked at many jobs, inspectors were afraid they would be unable to support themselves or their children, so a male relative or husband was required to accept them before they were released.

"Can you read?" was another question that could trip up children and some female immigrants who had never had the opportunity to attend school in their native lands. Uneducated immigrants faked it or were coached by others who had made it through the process.

Immigrant Aid Societies

Immigrant aid societies were organized for most countries and cultures that were represented at Ellis Island. Italian, Hebrew, Dutch, and Belgian groups and many other aid groups helped interpret languages for both immigrants and inspectors, provided temporary shelter for those with no contacts in America, directed immigrants toward legitimate employers, and stood beside detainees who went before the board of review at Ellis Island.

Medical Treatment

The United States government did pay for the medical treatment of detainees who were sick or had contagious diseases. During the sixty years Ellis Island was in operation, more than 350 babies were delivered. More than 3,500 immigrants died at Ellis Island. Doctors and nurses learned to treat diseases they had not encountered in America, many of which were the direct result of the conditions passengers faced on ships or contagious diseases that were common in the European countries from which they came.

FREE ADVICE

Reading Passages

Ellis Island:
Gateway to America *(cont.)*

Mail-Order Brides

Young, single men often went to America alone and soon found a real shortage of available young women who spoke their languages and belonged to their cultures. Many unmarried immigrant males paid for tickets for mail-order brides from their own countries. "Marriage agents" in Europe put unmarried women in contact with single men. Sometimes, the young brides-to-be were shocked by the looks of the prospective grooms, but most marriages actually worked out. One ship carried 1,200 would-be brides to America, causing a stir throughout the nation as young men went to Ellis Island in search of prospective wives.

Many young women did get detained at Ellis Island, waiting for husbands who failed to show. Ellis Island officials refused to release single women or married women, alone or with children, unless a father or husband came to claim them. They were afraid the women would be unable to find relatives in New York and be unable to support themselves.

Island of Tears, Island of Hope

Approximately fifteen million immigrants went through Ellis Island in the years from 1892 to 1954. More than one million went through in 1907, the peak year for immigration, and twelve million entered between 1892 and 1924. Somewhere between 200,000 and 300,000 immigrants were refused admittance and sent back to their native countries, sometimes on the same ships that brought them to America.

About seventy-nine out of every eighty immigrants did make it into America, representing almost 99% of the people who arrived on the ships. Approximately 100 million Americans out of the 300 million Americans alive today can trace their ancestry to one or more immigrants who came through Ellis Island. The American Immigrant Wall of Honor has hundreds of thousands of immigrant names inscribed in tribute to the men and women who endured the long ocean voyage, survived the entry inspections, and succeeded in America.

Reading Passages

Angel Island

Gold Mountain

The first Chinese immigrants came to America after the discovery of gold in California. The Chinese nickname for the United States was "Gum Saan," meaning Gold Mountain. That name stuck long after the California Gold Rush dwindled away. Millions of peasants in China were barely surviving in the provinces, and many made extreme sacrifices to come to America in the hope of striking it rich or just creating a better life for themselves and the families they hoped to send for later.

Most Chinese peasants made only about $20 a year in China. Passage to America cost $50. Those traveling to America borrowed the money when they could from relatives or merchants and then repaid it when they got work in America. These men traveled below decks in steerage and suffered greatly during the 50 to 100 days it took for the sailing ship to get to America. They had to sleep in shifts often sharing one bed. They had no water for washing and only a little fresh water for drinking. Crowding led to the spread of contagious illnesses and many deaths on board ship.

Working in America

Chinese miners were often cheated out of their gold by more ruthless prospectors and by special taxes imposed only on them by local authorities. Chinese men also found work in railroads, working for the Central Pacific Railroad and others, on farms and vineyards, as laundrymen, and in any other job they could get. Many whites resented them because they believed that the Chinese were taking their jobs and working for less pay. It is true that the Chinese were very hardworking and often would do work that whites considered too demeaning or low paying. The Chinese also started fishing and canning businesses and created a Chinese community called Chinatown in San Francisco with many small businesses.

Chinese workers began to be attacked by gangs of white men, and it became dangerous for them to be out at night. Chinese homes and businesses were destroyed, and their families were beaten and sometimes killed. Some Chinese fled from the West to eastern cities, but they were still targets of persecution.

Reading Passages

Angel Island (cont.)

The Burlingame Treaty

The United States signed the Burlingame Treaty in 1868 with China, which allowed citizens of both countries to travel back and forth as often as they liked. More than 300,000 Chinese laborers entered the United States between 1849, the start of the Gold Rush, and 1882, the passage of the Chinese Exclusion Act.

Chinese Exclusion Act

Because of complaints from white citizens, especially in California, the U.S. Congress passed the Chinese Exclusion Act of 1882, which excluded most Chinese laborers from entering the country for ten years. Diplomats, students, and highly educated Chinese were not included in the law, but it severely limited the Chinese workers who had come by the thousands in earlier years to work on the railroads, in mines, and on farms. Children born to Chinese living in the United States were still U.S. citizens. Chinese laborers living in the U.S. had to carry papers to prove they were entitled to live and work in the U.S.

"Paper Sons"

However, close family members of Chinese already in the country were still allowed to immigrate. Many Chinese men traveled to China and returned reporting that they had a new son. They established these "paper relatives" and then sold the papers to people who wished to immigrate. These immigrants became known as "paper sons" and "paper daughters."

The government quickly became aware of this deceptive practice and, in 1910, opened a formal immigration center on Angel Island in San Francisco Bay to process all immigrants from Asia. Some immigrants came from Japan, Korea, Russia, Australia, and other countries, but most of the detainees came from China.

The San Francisco earthquake and fire of 1906 destroyed all official immigration records in the Hall of Records, including those belonging to Chinese immigrants. Many Chinese residents used the fire to claim that they had proof of citizenship from the years before the exclusion act. Many Chinese claimed imaginary relatives, as well. Some sold these papers to Chinese immigrants hoping to enter the country. These "paper sons" were coached to answer questions from suspicious immigration agents, especially when new immigrants arrived at the facility at Angel Island.

Angel Island *(cont.)*

Guardian of the Western Gate

The nickname for Angel Island was "Guardian of the Western Gate," and for thirty years, it was the main processing center for immigrants arriving in the western United States. Angel Island Immigration Center was a series of buildings where immigrants were examined and questioned as at Ellis Island. Immigrants were immediately separated into three groups when they arrived at the examination center: whites, Japanese and other Asians, and Chinese. Most whites, Japanese, and other Asian immigrants were processed quickly and soon left the facility.

The Chinese immigrants were carefully examined for health problems because many were poor and sometimes had contagious diseases contracted in China or on board ships in the crowded conditions below decks. Then they had their papers examined and were carefully and rigorously questioned about the validity of their papers. Immigration officials were looking for "paper sons" and "paper daughters" among the immigrants. The questioning could last continuously for two or three days. Even legal immigrants had trouble remembering obscure facts about their villages or families.

Detainees

Legal and illegal immigrants were never certain if they passed and were often detained for long periods of time while officials decided if they could stay in America or had to return to China. Immigrants usually waited months for the results of the tests they had taken, although some immigrants had to wait as long as three years. Detainees lived in a two-story wooden barracks surrounded by barbed-wire fences and guards to keep them from escaping.

Reading Passages

Angel Island *(cont.)*

Conditions at Angel Island

The barracks were divided into two rooms with men sleeping in one room and women in the other. Each room contained rows of bunk beds. Often 70 to 100 men and women were detained at one time. Most of the day the detainees were locked in the barracks with a guard outside. The detainees were served two meals a day, but men and women ate at different times so that there was no communication between them. The immigrants complained that the food was poor. It was so bad in the early 1920s that food riots occurred.

During the long, boring days, immigrants played games, read newspapers and books, wrote letters, washed clothes, and napped. The immigrants could send and receive letters, but they were read by the authorities. Some immigrants sang or played musical instruments they had brought from China. Once a week, they were allowed outside to play ball in a small, fenced yard. Detainees were allowed to go to the docks once a week to take what they wanted from their luggage.

"The Angel of Angel Island"

The Women's Home Missionary Society sent Katherine Maurer to Angel Island to try to help the immigrants. She tried to make the immigrants more comfortable during their stay at the detention center. She brought toys for children and towels and soap for the adults of both genders. Katherine helped teach children and women to learn English and was called the "Angel of Angel Island" by the immigrants she helped for nearly thirty years.

Closed

One immigration official had called Angel Island a firetrap in 1922, and in 1940, fire did destroy the main building. The immigrants were moved to San Francisco, and Angel Island was never used again. Many of the Chinese immigrants had left poems expressing their feelings of loss, fear, and loneliness carved into the wooden walls. These poems have been saved, and Angel Island is now a California historic park open to visitors.

Reading Passages

The Fourth Wave (1945–Present)

War and Revolution

The period after World War II led to an increase in immigration due to the massive disruption in life caused by the war. The United States admitted the foreign wives and children of U.S. servicemen after World War II. Thousands of refugees from World War II, as well as refugees from communist revolutions in Cuba, China, and Eastern Europe, were also allowed to immigrate to the U.S. After World War II, the immigration laws were changed to allow U.S. citizenship to become available to all immigrants regardless of nationality or race.

Another New Immigration

In 1965, amendments to the immigration laws changed quotas based on nationality to quotas based on origin in either the Western or Eastern Hemisphere. The latest waves of immigration have come from Mexico, Cuba, the Philippines, other Middle American countries, China, Korea, India, other Asian nations, and Arab nations. Most of these new immigrants come for economic reasons, just as previous immigrants did, although some are fleeing political or religious oppression.

Legal and Illegal Immigration

Together, legal and illegal immigration has sent an average of one million immigrants a year to the United States since 1990. The United States gives preference in legal immigration to those who already have relatives and family in the country and those who have desirable education and job skills for the American workplace. Legal immigrants must still prove that they are not infectious disease carriers or convicted criminals. Over 100,000 legal immigrants come from Mexico each year, and approximately 50,000 each come from the Philippines, India, and China.

Modern Immigration

Immigrants still come to the United States in large numbers and for the same reasons as their predecessors. War, revolution, economic disasters, and opportunities for success and education propel immigrants to leave their homes and communities to seek a better life in the United States.

More than 700,000 refugees from Vietnam, Laos, and Cambodia entered the United States from 1975 to 1985 following the end of the Vietnam War and the violence that followed. Many Vietnamese were admitted after the war to protect those in Vietnam who had fought with the United States as an ally or who had worked with U.S. authorities.

Almost 500,000 immigrants have come from China in the last ten years, and about the same number have emigrated from the Philippines. About 600,000 have arrived from Korea and the same have arrived from India in the last ten years.

Reading Passages

The Fourth Wave (1945–Present) *(cont.)*

Mexican and Latin American Emigration

Emigration from Mexico, the Central American countries, and the Caribbean nations have provided the bulk of the immigrants in the last thirty-five years. Mexican immigrants had come in great numbers in the years between 1910 and the Great Depression, when many Mexicans were forcibly returned by the United States because of job competition with American citizens. However, the real migration came in the years after 1975 when political instability and poverty made life more difficult in Mexico. From 1976 to 1986, almost 750,000 immigrated to the U.S. About 1,800,000 have arrived in the last ten years, and about 9.6 million Mexican immigrants now live in the United States. Today, about 20 million Americans are of Mexican descent.

Almost 200,000 Cubans left their country during its revolution in the early 1960s. There have been several bursts of immigration when the Cuban government has allowed citizens to leave. About 1.1 million Cuban immigrants now live in the United States, many of them in Florida where they first arrived. Many emigrants also arrive each year from other Central American and Caribbean countries, such as El Salvador, Honduras, and the Dominican Republic.

Crossing the Border

Many people from Mexico walk across the largely unguarded border with the United States that extends from California to Texas. Although it is patrolled by agents of the Border Patrol and does have some fencing as obstruction, long stretches of the border are arid, empty, and largely uninhabited. Many people who are desperate for jobs or a better life hire "coyotes" to guide them and/or their children across to the States. They also illegally bring illegal immigrants across border checkpoints hidden in trucks and cars. Like those who preyed on earlier immigrants on the docks, these "coyotes" take advantage of the people they are supposed to guide into the country.

History Repeats Itself

Today's immigrants sometimes live in poor communities with others who share their culture, religion, and language. Fortunately, many immigrant children are in school and learning English. They become translators for their families, as they help them communicate with doctors, businesses, landlords, and even schools.

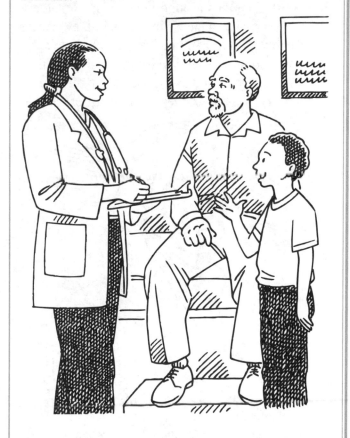

Reading Passages

Famous Immigrants, Part I

John Jacob Astor (1763–1848)

John Jacob Astor was born in Germany to the family of a poor butcher. He worked for his father as a young teen and went to London at the age of sixteen, where he learned English and earned enough money for passage to the United States in 1783. During the trip, his ship was stuck in ice for two months. Astor became interested in the fur trade in North America and worked for several fur companies.

Astor developed several business connections to sell furs purchased from American Indians to companies in England that would make the furs into hats and clothing. He acquired other businesses and a fleet of ships to quickly transport his goods around the world. He later developed many business interests in New York City, especially in banking, real estate, hotels, and railroad and canal development. His total wealth was estimated as high as thirty million dollars. He was the richest man in America.

Andrew Carnegie (1835–1919)

Andrew Carnegie was born in Scotland. His father was a weaver who lost his job with the invention of automatic machines that could weave cloth. His mother went to work and saved enough money to bring the family to Pittsburgh, Pennsylvania, where Andrew and his father got work at a cotton factory. Andrew made $1.20 a week. Later, he worked as a messenger boy in a telegraph office and then as a private secretary and telegraph operator for an executive. Andrew borrowed books from a local library and systematically studied business. He worked his way into better jobs managing the Pennsylvania Railroad.

Carnegie became involved in the iron business during the Civil War and later ran a bridge-making company. Carnegie recognized the benefits of a new steel-making process and invested heavily in this process, which worked very well. He built a steel company and was ruthless in keeping down costs, partly by keeping wages low. Carnegie became immensely rich. He had a reputation as a ruthless businessman who broke strikes and treated his workers poorly. Nonetheless, he also used his immense wealth to support many colleges, and he funded more than 2,500 public libraries after he sold his business. Carnegie was among the first to support the idea of a League of Nations to help preserve world peace. Carnegie was very opposed to the spread of war and deeply opposed to World War I.

Reading Passages

Famous Immigrants, Part I (cont.)

John Muir (1838–1914)

John Muir was born in Scotland and came to the United States when he was eleven years old. He lived on a farm in Wisconsin with his family and developed a deep love of nature and a fondness for making unique inventions, such as an early rising machine, a model sawmill, and a studying machine. He worked in several factories during the Civil War and was blinded in an accident. John gradually recovered and began a thousand-mile-long walk from Indianapolis, Indiana, to the Gulf Coast of Florida. After a bout with malaria, he sailed to San Francisco.

Muir walked into the Yosemite Valley and the Sierra Nevada Mountains where he climbed and explored extensively. He studied plants, wild animals, and even measured the movement of glaciers. He traveled to Alaska and studied glaciers. He campaigned for the creation of national parks, such as Yosemite National Park and Sequoia National Park. John Muir guided President Theodore Roosevelt through the Sierras and convinced him to establish a bureau of forestry to manage America's forests. In 1892, he founded the Sierra Club to advocate for the conservation of America's national resources. Muir became the symbol for modern conservationists. John Muir took extensive notes wherever he traveled. He wrote 300 articles and 10 books about nature.

Harry Houdini (1874–1926)

Harry Houdini was born Ehrich Weisz in Budapest, Hungary (although he often said he was born in the United States). At the age of four, he came to America with his Jewish family. His father was a rabbi who had difficulty finding a congregation that would keep him and pay him enough to support seven children. Ehrich worked on the street doing simple magic tricks, shining shoes, selling newspapers, and getting whatever money he could as a street actor. At the age of twelve, he ran away from home to make it easier for the rest of the family.

He was fascinated by magic. Eventually, he had read several books on the subject, adopted the name Harry Houdini, and begun putting on as many as twelve shows a day with his young wife. Harry developed a number of acts, such as swallowing needles, getting out of locked handcuffs, escaping from a straitjacket, escaping from a cell filled with water, and escaping from a sealed coffin, along with many others that made him the most prominent magician in the world. He died from a ruptured appendix.

Reading Passages

Famous Immigrants, Part I *(cont.)*

Enrico Fermi (1901–1954)

Enrico Fermi was a world-famous Italian nuclear scientist. He was proud of his Italian heritage but deeply worried about the behavior of Benito Mussolini who ruled Italy in the 1930s and who was setting up concentration camps for Jews in Italy. Enrico's wife was Jewish and Fermi knew that in a country controlled by Fascists, such as Mussolini, his family would always be in danger. There was no way he or his family would be able to immigrate. He was too famous, and the authorities would never allow him to leave. Enrico was the world's leading authority on neutrons, a kind of particle found in atoms.

However, in November 1938, Fermi received notification that he was invited to Stockholm in Sweden to receive the Nobel Prize in Physics. The Italian government, of course, wanted the prestige of an Italian receiving the award. He took his family to Sweden for the award ceremonies and then went directly to the United States where he had several offers to teach physics in college. He taught at Columbia University, developed the first controlled nuclear chain reaction, and worked on the Manhattan Project—the secret U.S. project to build the first atomic bomb. Fermi became an American citizen in 1944.

Golda Meir (1898–1978)

Golda Mabovitch (Meir) was a five-year-old girl when she, her parents, and her two sisters escaped from Russia. This country was ruled by a brutal czar. Golda and her family were always in danger from pogroms, which were organized attacks on Jewish families by peasants, that were then encouraged by the rulers. The family followed their father, a Jewish rabbi, to Milwaukee, Wisconsin. There, they lived and worked. Golda avoided an arranged marriage and joined her sister in Denver to complete high school. She became a firm believer in the idea of the Jewish nation of Israel. Although she had immigrated to America when she was eight, she left for the Jewish settlements in Palestine fifteen years later, having acquired an education, a husband, and a lifelong commitment to the cause of a nation for Jews. She would eventually become the first female Prime Minister in 1969. She served as Israel's leader until 1974 when she resigned at the age of seventy-six.

Reading
Passages

Famous Immigrants, Part II

Irving Berlin (1888–1989)

Israel Isidore Baline was born in a poverty-stricken Jewish ghetto in Russia. After their home was burned by marauding Cossack horsemen and with the hope to improve their lives, his family immigrated to the United States when he was five. Israel was the youngest of eight children. His father worked in low-paying jobs, and the older brothers and sisters also worked to support the family. So did Israel, who sold newspapers on the streets of New York. He learned songs in German, Irish, and Italian and sang them to attract attention to his papers. He later sang on the streets for pennies to help support the family.

After his father's death, Israel left home and school at fourteen to support himself. He started out singing songs in saloons for small change and became a "plugger," a singer who sang songs after a performance in a musical theater. Israel became a songwriter in 1907 and had his first hit, "Alexander's Ragtime Band," in 1911. The success of that song made him rich and famous. He invented a new name for himself that sounded more American and more memorable: Irving Berlin. During his service in the U.S. Army in World War I, Berlin wrote and directed a show by and for U.S. servicemen, which was very successful. After the war, many Broadway producers worked with Berlin, and he became very well known. His song "God Bless America" is one of the most popular American patriotic songs ever written.

Isaac Bashevis Singer (1904–1991)

Isaac Singer was born in Poland, the son of a rabbi. He grew up in Warsaw in a poor, Jewish section of the city and studied in a rabbinical seminary as a youth. Singer wrote in Yiddish, a Jewish language common to his people. Singer immigrated to the United States in 1935 because he recognized the dangers posed to all of Europe by the growth of Nazism in Germany. Singer wrote novels, several autobiographical works, and over 200 short stories. His books of children's stories are set in imaginary villages in Poland and based on people and ideas in Polish Jewish culture. His children's books, available in many libraries, include *Zlateh the Goat*, *When Shlemiel Went to Warsaw*, and *The Fools of Chelm*. Singer won the Nobel Prize for Literature in 1978.

Reading Passages

Famous Immigrants, Part II *(cont.)*

Felix Frankfurter (1882–1965)

Felix Frankfurter was born in Vienna, Austria. He emigrated from Austria with his parents when he was twelve years old to live in a crowded tenement in New York City. He worked his way through school, attended City College, and graduated from Harvard Law School. Frankfurter did some private-practice work, but he often worked in government offices, such as at the U.S. Attorney's office in Manhattan and as an assistant to the Secretary of War. He worked as a professor at Harvard Law School for more than twenty-five years. Frankfurter became famous as an expert in constitutional law.

Frankfurter argued cases for the National Consumers League, which was very concerned about causes supporting Jewish rights throughout the world, and helped create the magazine called *The New Republic*, which supported liberal causes. He defended two very unpopular men, accused of bank robbery and murder, who were committed for political reasons. Felix was a close friend of two famous Supreme Court Justices, Oliver Wendell Holmes Jr., and Louis Brandeis, and sent many of his Harvard students to work for them and for President Franklin Roosevelt, for whom he was an advisor. President Roosevelt appointed Frankfurter to the Supreme Court in 1938. He served until 1962. He is especially famous for his clear writing and legal opinions while on the Court.

Jaime Escalante (1930–2010)

Jaime Escalante was born in La Paz, Bolivia, where he was a good student. He was especially interested in math and science. He wanted to be an electrical engineer, but he did not have the money for college. He became a teacher in La Paz and got married. However, teaching was a poorly paid job in Bolivia, so he and his family moved to Pasadena, California, in 1963 where he had to learn English and take college courses for teaching in this country. After ten years of study and doing other jobs, Jaime became a teacher again at Garfield High School. He was forty-three when he began a long, successful career in helping previously underachieving students from poor backgrounds achieve success in math. He became famous for motivating and encouraging students to believe that they need to desire success in order to acquire it.

Reading Passages

Famous Immigrants, Part II *(cont.)*

Many Gifted Immigrants

A significant number of immigrants have graced America with their drive, courage, and determination to succeed.

Edward Teller, an immigrant from Hungary, was a major architect of the hydrogen bomb. Niels Bohr from Denmark came to America and worked on the first atomic bomb. Albert Einstein came to the U.S. from Germany to avoid the Nazi government of Adolph Hitler. His theory of relativity redefined the ideas of modern physics.

Architect I. M. Pei, born in Canton, China, came to the United States in 1935 to study architecture and became a U.S. citizen in 1954. He designed the entrance to the Louvre Museum in Paris, France; the John F. Kennedy Library; the East Building of the National Gallery of Art in Washington, D.C.; and the Rock and Roll Hall of Fame in Cleveland, Ohio.

Nikola Tesla immigrated to America from Croatia in 1884, having already done many experiments with electric currents and electric equipment. He worked for a time with Thomas Edison, although they violently disagreed over the correct current to use for electric equipment. Tesla's ideas about alternating current eventually won out. He had many electrical inventions, including one of the basic models for radio transmission.

Alexander Graham Bell emigrated from Scotland to Canada with his family, and then he came to Boston, Massachusetts, where he worked with deaf people. He was originally working on a device to help deaf people speak, when he became interested in the concept of transferring human speech electrically as the telegraph sends codes. He filed his patent for the telephone only hours before his rival, Elisha Gray, filed his patent for a similar invention. Bell won the battle in court and went on to experiment with planes, hydrofoils, tetrahedral kites, a telephone probe, a graphophone, and many other designs.

The First Wave (1600–1775) Quiz

Directions: Read pages 7–9 about the first wave of immigration to America. Answer these questions based on the information in the selection. Circle the correct answer to each question below. Underline the sentences in the reading selection where the answers are found.

1. About how many American Indians were living in the area now called the United States during the colonial period?

    a. one million

    b. ten million

    c. ten billion

    d. a few thousand

2. The first colonists came primarily from which continent?

    a. Asia

    b. Australia

    c. Europe

    d. all of the above

3. How many slaves came from Africa during the colonial period?

    a. three million

    b. several hundred

    c. 50,000

    d. 350,000

4. Which of these colonists were forced to immigrate to America?

    a. slaves

    b. convicts

    c. debtors

    d. all of the above

5. Which of these groups came to America to escape religious persecution?

    a. Quakers

    b. Catholics

    c. Puritans

    d. all of the above

6. How long did it take to make the ocean voyage across the Atlantic Ocean to America?

    a. ten months

    b. six to eight weeks

    c. eight to twelve weeks

    d. one year

7. Which disease of the teeth and mouth is caused by a lack of vitamins?

    a. scurvy

    b. dysentery

    c. seasickness

    d. lice

8. How many settlers lived in America in 1700?

    a. 400,000

    b. 350,000

    c. one million

    d. 250,000

9. How many European immigrants arrived in America between 1700 and 1775?

    a. 400,000

    b. 250,000

    c. six million

    d. 100,000

10. Why did 100,000 Irish settle in America during the colonial period?

    a. to escape poverty

    b. to own land

    c. to find better jobs

    d. all of the above

The Second Wave (1820–1870) Quiz

Directions: Read pages 10–13 about the second wave of immigration to America. Answer these questions based on the information in the selection. Circle the correct answer to each question below. Underline the sentences in the reading selection where the answers are found.

1. Which was the major port of entry into the United States for immigrants coming between 1820 and 1870?
   a. Philadelphia
   b. New York
   c. Chicago
   d. Los Angeles

2. Who would sell cheap land to immigrants?
   a. railroads
   b. the federal government
   c. New York City
   d. both a and b

3. What is the meaning of the word "sojourners"?
   a. starvation
   b. persecution
   c. famine
   d. travelers

4. How many Irish immigrated to the United States during the years of the potato famine?
   a. more than 7.5 million
   b. more than one million
   c. less than 500,000
   d. less than 200,000

5. What was Castle Garden?
   a. a state immigration center
   b. a model farm
   c. a millionaire's garden
   d. an amusement park

6. Where did steerage passengers travel on the ship?
   a. on the top deck
   b. in the crew's quarters
   c. below deck
   d. all of the above

7. Which of the following problems affected steerage passengers?
   a. rotten food
   b. poor opportunities for hygiene
   c. contagious diseases
   d. all of the above

8. Which word describes people with no money or valuables?
   a. destitute
   b. sojourners
   c. official
   d. famine

9. Where did the Chinese usually immigrate to in America?
   a. Wisconsin
   b. California
   c. New York
   d. New England

10. Which two countries were each the source of 2.5 million immigrants between 1820 and 1870?
    a. Ireland and Poland
    b. Canada and China
    c. Germany and Scotland
    d. Ireland and Germany

The Third Wave (1880–1920) Quiz

Directions: Read pages 14–16 about the third wave of immigration to America. Answer these questions based on the information in the selection. Circle the correct answer to each question below. Underline the sentences in the reading selection where the answers are found.

1. Where did the new immigrants largely come from in the years from 1880 to 1920?
   a. Great Britain
   b. northern and western Europe
   c. China
   d. southern and eastern Europe

2. Which of these countries was not a major source of immigration to America during this wave of immigration?
   a. Russia
   b. India
   c. Poland
   d. Italy

3. Which of these reasons caused people to immigrate to America during this period?
   a. political persecution
   b. religious persecution
   c. economic needs
   d. all of the above

4. What did English-speaking children do to help their parents?
   a. They became family translators.
   b. They drove taxis.
   c. They taught school.
   d. They became landlords.

5. Where did some immigrant children work?
   a. coal mines
   b. textile factories
   c. on farms
   d. all of the above

6. Educated immigrant women worked in all of these jobs except
   a. offices.
   b. skyscraper construction.
   c. telephone companies.
   d. retail stores.

7. What word means "a limit placed on a number of people"?
   a. undesirable
   b. landlord
   c. quota
   d. tenement

8. How many people might be living in a single block of tenements?
   a. ten
   b. four million
   c. 32
   d. 4,000

9. What does a textile factory work with?
   a. food
   b. cloth
   c. construction
   d. coal

10. Which of the following did not slow immigration from 1880–1920?
    a. Chinese Exclusion Act
    b. immigration restrictions
    c. rise of skyscrapers
    d. immigration quotas

Ellis Island: Gateway to America Quiz

Directions: Read pages 17–21 about Ellis Island. Answer these questions based on the information in the selection. Circle the correct answer to each question below. Underline the sentences in the reading selection where the answers are found.

1. How many acres did the immigration center at Ellis Island contain?
   a. three
   b. $27\frac{1}{2}$
   c. six
   d. 400

2. What did the chalk letters "SC" on an immigrant's clothes stand for?
   a. heart defect
   b. hernia
   c. scalp disease
   d. serious cancer

3. On what day did fire completely destroy the buildings?
   a. June 14, 1897
   b. January 1, 1892
   c. June 15, 1897
   d. December 31, 1954

4. How many living Americans can trace their ancestry to an immigrant who entered America through Ellis Island?
   a. 300 million
   b. 15 million
   c. 100 million
   d. 300,000

5. How many immigrants died at Ellis Island?
   a. 3,500
   b. 350
   c. 24 million
   d. none

6. What contagious eye disease did inspectors look for?
   a. smallpox
   b. typhoid fever
   c. lice
   d. trachoma

7. Which immigrants were considered "undesirable" and needed to be carefully inspected?
   a. the mentally unfit
   b. the physically handicapped
   c. the Ellis Island officials
   d. both a and b

8. Which of these things did immigrant aid societies do?
   a. interpret languages
   b. help detainees
   c. help immigrants find jobs
   d. all of the above

9. Which of these groups could not be released from Ellis Island until a man accepted them?
   a. teenagers
   b. women traveling alone
   c. mothers with children
   d. both b and c

10. Approximately how many immigrants entered America through Ellis Island?
    a. 15 million
    b. one million
    c. 300,000
    d. 100 million

Angel Island Quiz

Directions: Read pages 22–25 about Angel Island. Answer these questions based on the information in the selection. Circle the correct answer to each question below. Underline the sentences in the reading selection where the answers are found.

1. What did the nickname "Gum Saan" mean?
   a. good-bye
   b. Gold Mountain
   c. Angel Island
   d. both b and c

2. What destroyed all of the Chinese immigration records?
   a. floods
   b. earthquake
   c. volcanic eruption
   d. prairie fire

3. When was Angel Island opened as an immigration center?
   a. 1910
   b. during the Gold Rush
   c. 1906
   d. 1940

4. Who was the "Angel of Angel Island"?
   a. Gum Saan
   b. a paper daughter
   c. Katherine Maurer
   d. a ghost that haunted the island

5. What jobs did Chinese workers hold?
   a. railroad workers
   b. laundrymen
   c. miners
   d. all of the above

6. Why were Chinese workers excluded from entering America in the Chinese Exclusion Act of 1882?
   a. They wouldn't work.
   b. White workers complained.
   c. They couldn't find jobs.
   d. They made too much money.

7. Most detainees at Angel Island came from which country?
   a. Japan
   b. United States
   c. China
   d. all of the above

8. Which of these features were present at the barracks where detainees were kept?
   a. barbed wire
   b. guards
   c. locked barracks
   d. all of the above

9. What were Chinese immigrants checked for at Angel Island?
   a. contagious diseases
   b. valid papers and documents
   c. work skills
   d. both a and b

10. What couldn't detainees at Angel Island do every day?
    a. write letters
    b. play musical instruments
    c. read books and papers
    d. go outside to play ball

The Fourth Wave (1945–Present) Quiz

Directions: Read pages 26–27 about the fourth wave of immigration to America. Answer these questions based on the information in the selection. Circle the correct answer to each question below. Underline the sentences in the reading selection where the answers are found.

1. What is the average number of legal and illegal immigrants coming into the United States each year since 1990?
   a. one million
   b. 100,000
   c. 9.6 million
   d. 700,000

2. Legal immigrants must prove that they are not
   a. convicted criminals.
   b. infectious disease carriers.
   c. doctors or lawyers.
   d. both a and b

3. About 600,000 immigrants have come to the United States from each of which two countries in the last ten years?
   a. India and Korea
   b. China and Austria
   c. Canada and Ireland
   d. Cuba and Vietnam

4. About how many Mexican immigrants now live in the United States?
   a. 1,800,000
   b. 9.6 million
   c. 20 million
   d. 750,000

5. What is the name given to people who illegally guide illegal Mexican immigrants into the United States across the border?
   a. coyotes
   b. wolves
   c. mules
   d. both a and b

6. From which two countries have about 500,000 immigrants arrived in the last ten years?
   a. Mexico and Honduras
   b. Vietnam and Japan
   c. Korea and Cuba
   d. China and the Philippines

7. How many Cubans left their country in the early 1960s?
   a. almost 800,000
   b. more than 220,000
   c. nearly 200,000
   d. more than 350,000

8. How do many modern immigrant children help their families?
   a. work in mines
   b. become translators for parents
   c. sell newspapers on streets
   d. join gangs

9. Who did the United States allow to immigrate after World War II?
   a. refugees from China
   b. foreign wives and children of U.S. servicemen
   c. refugees from Eastern Europe
   d. all of the above

10. What problems in their native countries caused immigrants to come to the United States during this period?
    a. war
    b. revolution
    c. severe economic problems
    d. all of the above

Famous Immigrants, Part I Quiz

Directions: Read pages 28–30 about famous immigrants. Answer these questions based on the information in the selection. Circle the correct answer to each question below. Underline the sentences in the reading selection where the answers are found.

1. Which immigrant from Scotland funded the building of more than 2,500 public libraries?
    a. John Jacob Astor
    b. Enrico Fermi
    c. Andrew Carnegie
    d. John Muir

2. Which immigrant from Hungary became a famous showman and magician?
    a. Harry Houdini
    b. Golda Meir
    c. John Muir
    d. Enrico Fermi

3. Which Jewish immigrant came first to the United States and later immigrated to Israel?
    a. Enrico Fermi
    b. Andrew Carnegie
    c. Golda Meir
    d. John Muir

4. What country did John Muir and Andrew Carnegie emigrate from?
    a. Ireland
    b. England
    c. Scotland
    d. France

5. Who was born with the name Ehrich Weisz?
    a. Golda Meir
    b. Harry Houdini
    c. Enrico Fermi
    d. John Muir

6. Which immigrant founded the Sierra Club to advocate for the conservation of America's natural resources?
    a. John Muir
    b. Andrew Carnegie
    c. Golda Meir
    d. Harry Houdini

7. Which immigrant developed the first controlled nuclear chain reaction?
    a. Albert Einstein
    b. Enrico Fermi
    c. Andrew Carnegie
    d. John Muir

8. Which immigrant had a father who was a Jewish rabbi?
    a. Enrico Fermi
    b. Golda Meir
    c. Harry Houdini
    d. both b and c

9. Who won the Nobel Prize in Physics and used the trip to Sweden as a chance to escape to America with his family?
    a. Enrico Fermi
    b. Albert Einstein
    c. Andrew Carnegie
    d. Golda Meir

10. Which fur trader and New York businessman became the richest man in America?
    a. John Jacob Astor
    b. Harry Houdini
    c. Andrew Carnegie
    d. John Muir

Famous Immigrants, Part II Quiz

Directions: Read pages 31–33 about famous immigrants. Answer these questions based on the information in the selection. Circle the correct answer to each question below. Underline the sentences in the reading selection where the answers are found.

1. Which immigrant from Austria became a United States Supreme Court Justice?
   a. Irving Berlin
   b. Isaac Bashevis Singer
   c. Felix Frankfurter
   d. Nikola Tesla

2. Which immigrant from Croatia worked on experiments with electricity?
   a. Thomas Edison
   b. Nikola Tesla
   c. Alexander Graham Bell
   d. Irving Berlin

3. Which Polish immigrant wrote books and stories for children and adults?
   a. Irving Berlin
   b. Isaac Bashevis Singer
   c. Edward Teller
   d. Jaime Escalante

4. Which Russian immigrant wrote "God Bless America"?
   a. Felix Frankfurter
   b. Isaac Bashevis Singer
   c. Irving Berlin
   d. Edward Teller

5. Which Scottish immigrant experimented with hydrofoils, kites, and planes?
   a. Irving Berlin
   b. Alexander Graham Bell
   c. Felix Frankfurter
   d. Nikola Tesla

6. Which immigrant became a famous math teacher for high school students?
   a. Edward Teller
   b. Alexander Graham Bell
   c. Jaime Escalante
   d. Felix Frankfurter

7. Which of these jobs was not held by Felix Frankfurter?
   a. Harvard professor
   b. advisor to President Roosevelt
   c. sheriff
   d. all of the above

8. Which famous architect was born in Canton, China?
   a. Niels Bohr
   b. I. M. Pei
   c. Edward Teller
   d. Isaac Bashevis Singer

9. Which of these immigrants came from Denmark and worked on the first atomic bomb?
   a. Edward Teller
   b. Niels Bohr
   c. Albert Einstein
   d. Nikola Tesla

10. Which country did the designer of the John F. Kennedy Library come from?
    a. Hungary
    b. China
    c. Scotland
    d. France

Teacher Lesson Plans for Language Arts

Vocabulary

Objective: Students will expand their knowledge of words and terms associated with immigration.

Materials: copies of The Language of Immigration (page 45), Immigration Crossword Puzzle (page 46), American Words Taken from Other Languages (page 47), and American Idioms (page 48); Glossary (page 93) (optional)

Procedure

1. Reproduce and distribute The Language of Immigration and the Immigration Crossword Puzzle. Review the words with students. Have students complete the pages independently. They may want to refer to the reading passages in this book or the Glossary.

2. Reproduce and distribute American Words Taken from Other Languages and American Idioms. Review the new words and the meanings of the idioms with the students. Have students complete the pages independently.

Assessment: Correct each worksheet and review the meanings of the words and idioms with the class.

Newspapers

Objective: Students will learn to apply their language arts skills in using newspapers and writing a newspaper.

Materials: copies of Immigrant News (page 49) and Create Your Own Newspaper (page 50); newspapers and Internet newspapers

Procedure

1. Reproduce and distribute Immigrant News. Have students read the page independently. Review the assignment. Distribute copies of newspapers. Have students use newspapers to complete the tasks on page 49.

2. Reproduce and distribute Create Your Own Newspaper. Have students get into small groups (four to six students each) and create a newspaper using the directions on page 50.

Assessment: Review each newspaper with the student teams for accuracy and completion of assignment.

Teacher Lesson Plans for Language Arts *(cont.)*

Working with Fact Sources

Objective: Students will learn to apply their language arts skills in using almanacs and encyclopedias.

Materials: copies of Working with Fact Sources: Almanacs (pages 51 and 52) and Working with Fact Sources: Encyclopedias (page 53); almanacs, encyclopedias, and Internet sources

Procedure

Note: You may wish to do these assignments as independent projects, depending on how many sources you have.

1. Reproduce and distribute Working with Fact Sources: Almanacs. Have students read the directions and assignments independently or together as a class.

2. Distribute copies of almanacs or use Internet access. Review the assignment with the class and help students get started.

3. Reproduce and distribute Working with Fact Sources: Encyclopedias. Read the assignment with the students and help them find sources.

Assessment: Have students share facts or exchange fact sheets.

Literature

Objective: Students will read from and respond to literature in the form of historical novels.

Materials: copies of Focus on an Author: Pam Muñoz Ryan (page 54), Read and Respond: *Esperanza Rising* (page 55), Read and Respond: *Letters from Rifka* (page 56), and Read and Respond: *Ashes of Roses* (page 57); copies of listed novels

Procedure

1. Reproduce and distribute Focus on an Author: Pam Muñoz Ryan and Read and Respond: *Esperanza Rising*. Discuss the author and her work. Assign *Esperanza Rising* to the class. Have students answer the questions before meeting in small groups or as a class to discuss the text and share responses.

2. Reproduce and distribute Read and Respond: *Letters from Rifka*. Assign *Letters from Rifka* to the class. Have students answer the questions before meeting in small groups or as a class to discuss the text and share responses. Encourage students to share their favorite passages.

3. Reproduce and distribute Read and Respond: *Ashes of Roses*. Assign *Ashes of Roses* to the class. Have students prepare the plot outline and answer the questions before meeting in small groups or as a class to discuss the text and share responses. Encourage students to share their personal reflections on the text.

Assessment: Use student worksheets and class discussions to assess students' performance on the literature selections.

Teacher Lesson Plans for Language Arts *(cont.)*

Diaries

Objective: Students will read from and respond to literature in the form of diaries.

Materials: copies of Read and Respond: *Hope in My Heart* (page 58), Immigrant Diaries (pages 59–60), Create Your Own Diary (page 61); copies of *Hope in My Heart: Sophia's Immigrant Diary*

Procedure

1. Reproduce and distribute Read and Respond: *Hope in My Heart*. Assign *Hope in My Heart: Sophia's Immigrant Diary* to the class. Have students answer the questions before meeting in small groups or as a class to discuss the text and share responses.

2. Reproduce and distribute Immigrant Diaries. Assign diaries to the class. Have students answer the questions before meeting in small groups or as a class to discuss the texts and share responses.

3. Reproduce and distribute Create Your Own Diary. Encourage each student to create and maintain a diary.

Assessment: Use student activity pages and diaries, as well as class discussions to assess students' performance on the literature selections.

Readers' Theater

Objective: Students will learn to use their voices effectively in dramatic reading.

Materials: copies of Readers' Theater Notes (page 62), Background Information: Albert Einstein (page 63), Readers' Theater: Relativity! Relativity! Relativity! (pages 64–65)

Procedure

1. Reproduce and distribute Readers' Theater Notes. Review the basic concepts of Readers' Theater with the class.

2. Reproduce and distribute Background Information: Albert Einstein and script of Relativity! Relativity! Relativity! Arrange students in small groups and allow them time over several days to practice reading the background information and the script together.

3. Schedule class performances, and have students share the prepared script.

4. Use the suggestions in the Extension activity at the bottom of page 62 to allow students to write their own Readers' Theater. Assign topics to teams of students, or let them choose their own. Allow time for them to create and practice their scripts.

5. Schedule classroom performances of these scripts, or invite another class to view the productions.

Assessment: Base performance assessments on pacing, volume, expression, and focus of the participants. Student-created scripts should demonstrate general writing skills, dramatic tension, and a good plot.

| 1600 | 1650 | 1700 | 1750 | 1800 | 1850 | 1900 | 1950 | 2000 |

The Language of Immigration

Directions: Use the words from the Word Bank to complete the sentences below. The meanings of the words are listed in the Glossary.

Word Bank

apprentice	emigrant	indentured servant
assimilate	epidemic	melting pot
competition	exclusion	persecution
convict	famine	port of entry
debtor	immigration	poverty

1. Many immigrants from England were fleeing religious _____ when they came to America.

2. An _____ might have to be an unpaid laborer for seven years or more.

3. New York City was the _____ for many newly arrived immigrants in America.

4. Historians often say the United States is a _____ with many people from many countries and cultures.

5. A _____ is a period of hunger caused by a shortage of food.

6. A _____ is someone who owes money he cannot repay.

7. A policy of _____ limits the entrance into the country of people from a specific race, country, religion, or culture.

8. When there is too much _____ for jobs, pay goes down.

9. A person in prison is called a _____.

10. A person living in _____ has no money or income.

11. An _____ learns a job by working for a person skilled in that occupation.

12. When a disease spreads quickly to many people, it becomes an _____.

13. Americans wanted immigrants to _____ into the American culture by learning the language and traditions of their new country.

14. The movement into a new country is called _____.

15. A person moving out of a country or area is called an _____.

1600 1650 1700 1750 1800 1850 1900 1950 2000

Immigration Crossword Puzzle

Directions: Use the words in the Word Bank to complete the puzzle. The meanings of the words are listed in the Glossary.

Word Bank

alien

emigrant

famine

indentured

melting pot

passport

pogrom

port

poverty

propaganda

quarantine

steerage

tenements

trachoma

undocumented

vermin

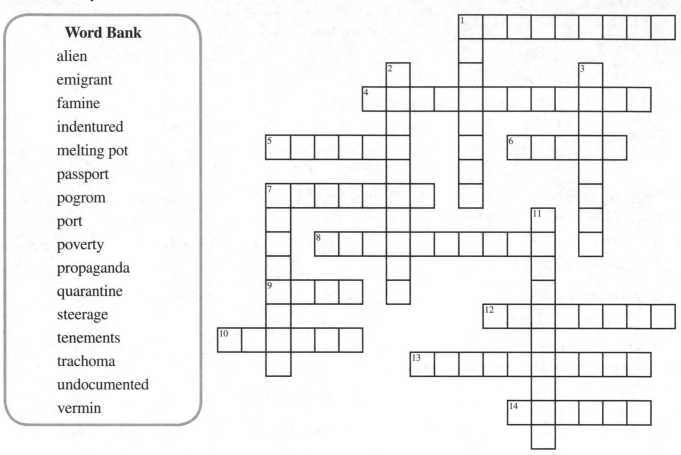

Across

1. crowded apartments in cities
4. illegal alien
5. extreme shortage of food
6. person from another country
7. having no money or resources
8. separating sick people
9. place where immigrants' ships arrived
10. unwanted mice or insects
12. person leaving a country
13. misleading ideas
14. organized massacre of people for religious reasons

Down

1. contagious eye disease
2. person who sells himself to get to America
3. poor class of travel below decks
7. form allowing a person to enter
11. one culture formed from many

American Words Taken from Other Languages

American English often borrows and adapts words and phrases from other languages. Some of these words come from languages used by immigrants.

Directions: Use a dictionary to help you match the Words/Phrases with the Meanings. Then write the language that each term comes from on the lines. The first one has been done for you.

Language	Word/Phrase	Meaning
1. _____French_____	savoir faire	a social mistake
2. _____	hoi polloi	common people
3. _____	enfant terrible	compared with
4. _____	fatwa	full power to act
5. _____	fait accompli	a person who likes expensive food
6. _____	bon vivant	smooth social skills
7. _____	boondocks	Japanese animation
8. _____	bodega	a done deal
9. _____	intelligentsia	rude person or child
10. _____	anime	intellectual group
11. _____	alfresco	grocery store
12. _____	vis-à-vis	rural area
13. _____	mensch	an inferior substitute
14. _____	cognoscente	newly rich
15. _____	ersatz	outdoors
16. _____	carte blanche	an honorable person
17. _____	faux pas	a religious command
18. _____	nouveau riche	joy of living
19. _____	joie de vivre	a confrontation
20. _____	mano a mano	an expert

American Idioms

An *idiom* is a phrase with a different meaning than what it literally says. Many immigrants learning a new language are often confused by American idioms.

Example: "I got it straight from the horse's mouth" means that you heard information from the real source of a story, not that a horse talked to you.

Directions: Write the real meaning of each underlined idiom on the lines below.

1. Jerry and Kim decided to <u>paint the town red</u>.

   Meaning: _____

2. Mary and Cho decided <u>to give</u> Jackie <u>the slip</u>.

   Meaning: _____

3. Joseph and James were <u>up a creek without a paddle</u>.

   Meaning: _____

4. Aaron had <u>to pay through the nose</u> for a new computer.

   Meaning: _____

5. Charles bought a car, but it turned out to be a <u>lemon</u>.

   Meaning: _____

6. "Stop <u>pulling my leg</u>," Ray told Anthony.

   Meaning: _____

7. Matilda was <u>talking through her hat</u> when she said she made a million cupcakes for the party.

   Meaning: _____

8. John is <u>at the end of his rope</u> trying to get his baby sister to eat her peas.

   Meaning: _____

9. Elena decided <u>to take the bull by the horns</u> when her sister listened in on her phone call.

   Meaning: _____

10. Olivia <u>smelled a rat</u> when her brother asked to borrow her bike.

    Meaning: _____

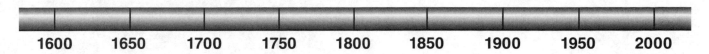

Immigrant News

Newspapers were often the major source of information for immigrants. People who could read English shared the news with less literate friends. Children educated in public schools read the papers and often translated the news for elders. Many immigrant boys, especially those who were very poor, often sold the papers on the streets and shouted out headlines. Some newspapers were also written in the native languages of the immigrants.

Assignment

1. Examine the sections of any newspaper. You may want to use a local newspaper or a big-city newspaper, like the *New York Times*. You can also find many city newspapers posted on the Internet.
2. Find and identify the sections of a newspaper listed below.
3. Skim, or quickly read, each section listed.
4. Describe what kind of information is contained in each section listed below.

Newspaper Sections

Front Page—top—the most important news of the day

_____

_____

Below the Fold—front page, bottom—important news

_____

_____

Local News—news about your city or town

_____

_____

National and International News

_____

_____

Business and Stock Market

_____

_____

Sports—local and national sporting events

_____

_____

Editorial Page—opinions of editors and readers

_____

_____

Obituary Notices—who died

_____

_____

Create Your Own Newspaper

Assignment

1. Form a small group of four to six students. You are now a team of reporters that will create a newspaper.

2. Listen to one local radio or television newscast and one national news report. If needed, consult newspapers, Internet news reports, and other broadcasts.

3. Take notes briefly but clearly about each of the topics listed below. Get the facts and write fast. Keep your notes organized by topic.

Newspaper Topics

The World

What's happening in the world—wars, revolutions, earthquakes and natural disasters, worldwide epidemics, international economic problems

The Nation

What's happening in the United States—presidential and congressional actions and laws, elections, natural disasters, such as floods, hurricanes, tornadoes, and blizzards

Local News

What's happening in your state and local city or town—actions of the governor, state assembly, or city council, new businesses, local and state school news, crimes, local accomplishments

Entertainment

Movies, television shows, new music releases, star notes, popular games

Business

New products, the national economy, successful business ideas, stock market news, jobs, unemployment figures

Sports

National sports and championships, local professional teams, college sports, and local school sporting events

Obituaries

Notices about the deaths of important people, celebrities, and local residents

Going to Press

1. Choose an editor to lead the team and organize the newspaper.

2. Assign individual reporters for each topic to put together all the notes and write the articles.

3. The editor will proofread each article for punctuation and grammar.

4. Each reporter can input his or her final stories.

5. Print the newspaper. Copy and distribute the paper to classmates and the teacher.

Working with Fact Sources: Almanacs

Almanacs are books that contain millions of facts on subjects as different as nations, states, presidents, world leaders, sports, science and inventions, actors, and many other areas of interest.

Assignment

1. Select an almanac with a large variety of factual information about the world, such as *The World Almanac*.

2. Make a list of twelve topics included in the almanac. Write the page number next to the topic.

	Topic	Page		Topic	Page
1.	_____	_____	7.	_____	_____
2.	_____	_____	8.	_____	_____
3.	_____	_____	9.	_____	_____
4.	_____	_____	10.	_____	_____
5.	_____	_____	11.	_____	_____
6.	_____	_____	12.	_____	_____

Pick a Topic

Directions: Choose one of the topics you listed that interests you. It may have interesting facts, statistics that impress you, or be related to something you have read. Then list six interesting facts about the topic you chose.

Your Topic: _____

1. _____

   _____

2. _____

   _____

3. _____

   _____

4. _____

   _____

5. _____

   _____

6. _____

   _____

Working with Fact Sources: Almanacs *(cont.)*

Assignment

1. Select an almanac, encyclopedia, or Internet site related to nations of the world.
2. Choose one of the nations from which people have immigrated to the United States.
3. Find the information listed below, and complete your Nation Fact Page.

Nation Fact Page

Population

Number of people: _____

Principal language spoken: _____

Other languages spoken: _____

Geography

Total area (square miles): _____

Location (continent): _____

Neighboring countries: _____

Capital city: _____

Government

Type of government: _____

Economy

Chief crops grown: _____

Industries (products made): _____

Natural resources: _____

Transportation

Types of public transportation: _____

Number of motor vehicles: _____

Education

Literacy (percentage of people who can read and write): _____

Health

Life expectancy: Male _____ Female _____

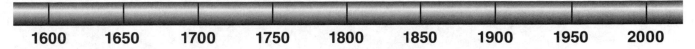

Working with Fact Sources: Encyclopedias

Assignment

1. Select an encyclopedia that lists information about each state of the United States. Remember that encyclopedias are organized alphabetically. (You can also find this information in almanacs and on the Internet.)

2. Choose one of the states to where people have immigrated.

3. Find the information listed below, and complete your State Fact Page.

State Fact Page

Population

Number of people: _____

Rank in size by number of people: _____

Percentage of people in urban (city) areas: _____

Percentage of people in rural areas: _____

Geography

Total area (square miles): _____

Neighboring states: _____

Capital city: _____

Major cities: _____

Government

Electoral votes (for president): _____

Economy

Chief crops grown: _____

Industries (products made): _____

Natural resources: _____

Special Facts

Statehood date: _____

Postal abbreviation: _____

State motto: _____

State bird: _____

State flower: _____

Focus on an Author: Pam Muñoz Ryan

Pam Muñoz Ryan was born and raised in the San Joaquin Valley of California, the oldest of three girls and the oldest of twenty-three grandchildren. She was also older than the three neighbor girls who lived near her. Because of her age, Ryan often took charge of what they did. She directed the games they played, acted as the pretend mother, became the heroine of their imaginations, and was generally the person in charge. She believes that this role helped prepare her for her life as a writer.

Ryan has a multi-ethnic background, including Spanish, Mexican, Basque (an ethnic community in Spain), and Italian. The summers were so hot in the valley that she often rode her bike to the public library because it was air-conditioned. As a child, she read the *Little House* books by Laura Ingalls Wilder, series books with girl heroines, and classics, such as *Treasure Island* and *The Swiss Family Robinson*. She also read *Gone with the Wind* in junior high school. Ryan became a grade-school teacher partly because she liked books. After marriage and four children, she was getting her master's degree when a professor asked if she had thought of becoming a writer. Then a friend asked her to help her write a book.

Pam Muñoz Ryan discovered that she did indeed enjoy writing and used her personal experiences and those of her family as the subjects of her stories. She has written many award-winning stories for young children that are set in the Mexican American heritage of her upbringing. The story of *Esperanza Rising* is based on her grandmother's life. She was named Esperanza, and she left Mexico to work on the farms in California. Her grandmother was already married, and Ryan's mother was born in the work camps. Many of the events described in the story happened to her grandmother and their family and friends. The author even has a natural immunity to Valley Fever because she grew up where it was so common.

Ryan also took many of the idioms and sayings used in *Esperanza Rising* from her special memories of conversations with her grandmother and her mother, Esperanza Muñoz. Ryan had heard many of the stories from her family of their life in the camps and their fear of being picked up and deported to Mexico. Somewhere between 450,000 and 1,000,000 people of Mexican heritage were deported during the Depression years, including many United States citizens of Mexican descent who had never lived in Mexico.

Pam Muñoz Ryan's books include:

Riding Freedom
Becoming Naomi Leon
Paint the Wind
Esperanza Rising

Read and Respond: *Esperanza Rising*

Esperanza Rising is set during the beginning of the Great Depression when many Mexican laborers immigrated to California looking for work in farm labor camps. There were many Asian workers and "Okies" from the American Midwest competing for the same jobs.

Assignment

1. Read Focus on an Author: Pam Muñoz Ryan (page 54).

2. Read *Esperanza Rising* by Pam Muñoz Ryan.

3. Answer the questions below, and share your responses in a small group or class discussion.

Comprehension Questions

1. Why do Esperanza and her mother have to leave Mexico?

2. How does Esperanza embarrass her mother on the train when the poor child wants to touch her doll?

3. What illness does Esperanza's mom get? What happens to the mother?

4. Why does Miguel take the money orders? What is the money being saved for?

5. Why does Abuelita have to be so careful in coming to America? Who is trying to find her? Where has she hidden?

6. What gift does Esperanza give Isabel?

Discussion Starters

1. Why doesn't Isabel win Queen of the May?

2. Who is probably responsible for the death of Esperanza's father?

3. What kinds of discrimination do the Mexican immigrants encounter?

4. How does the author count the passage of time for each chapter?

5. How do you know that Esperanza's father and mother must have been kind to Hortensia and her family when they lived in Mexico?

6. Why can't Esperanza and her mother support Marta and the union?

7. How does Esperanza change over time from the beginning to the end of the book?

8. What do you think will happen to Esperanza in the future?

Making It Personal

1. What are your personal feelings about the book?

2. Who was your favorite character? Why?

3. Would you like to read the book again sometime? Why?

4. Would you like to read other books by the same author?

Read and Respond: *Letters from Rifka*

Letters from Rifka is a novel written in the form of a series of letters from a girl immigrating to America from Russia in 1919. The novel is based on the true experiences of the author's great aunt who fled Russia with her Jewish family in the post World War I years to avoid the pogroms inflicted by the Soviet government upon the Jews.

Assignment

1. Read *Letters from Rifka* by Karen Hesse.
2. Answer the questions below, and share your responses in a small group or class discussion.

Discussion Starters

1. Why does Rifka's family decide to leave Russia?
2. Why do Uncle Avrum, Tovah, and their family not leave Russia?
3. Why is the book of poetry by Pushkin so important to Rifka?
4. What dangers and terrible events do Rifka and her family encounter during the escape from Russia through Poland?
5. Why can't the family return to Russia? What could happen to them and Tovah's family?
6. What special skills does Rifka have that enrich her life and help others?
7. How does Rifka get ringworm?
8. Why are Rifka's experiences in Antwerp so valuable to her growth as a person?
9. How does Rifka help Ilya and other detainees at Ellis Island?
10. Why do you think Ilya doesn't talk with the adults at Ellis Island?
11. What does Mr. Fargate find amusing and admirable about Rifka?
12. Describe Rifka's relationship with her brother, Saul.

Making It Personal

1. What do you like or dislike about the personality and character of Rifka?
2. What did you learn about the history and process of immigration and the character of the immigrants from the book?
3. What do you think was the worst thing that happened to Rifka? Explain your answer.
4. What did you think or feel about the poetic passages from Pushkin quoted at the beginning of each chapter?

Passages to Share

Find two lines or paragraphs that you liked from the book to share with your classmates.

1. Page: _____ Beginning words: _____

   Reason for choice: _____

2. Page: _____ Beginning words: _____

   Reason for choice: _____

Read and Respond: *Ashes of Roses*

Ashes of Roses is a historical novel set in New York City in 1911–1912 at the time of the Triangle Shirtwaist Factory disaster. It is the story of an immigrant girl from Ireland trying to survive and succeed in her new country.

Assignment

1. Read *Ashes of Roses* by Mary Jane Auch.
2. Complete the Plot Outline on this page.
3. Answer the questions below, and share your responses in a small group or class discussion.

Plot Outline

List ten important plot events that happen to Rose in the story.

1. _____
2. _____
3. _____
4. _____
5. _____
6. _____
7. _____
8. _____
9. _____
10. _____

Discussion Starters

1. Does Rose make the right decision to stay in America? Why?
2. Why are the girls in the Triangle Shirtwaist Factory locked in during work hours?
3. Who do you think teaches Rose the most about surviving in America?
4. What lessons about living in America does Rose learn?
5. Why does Patrick's wife dislike Rose and her family?
6. What countries or cultures are represented by the people Rose encounters and works with?

Making It Personal

1. What do you most admire about Rose's personality or character?
2. What is the best decision Rose makes? Why?
3. What is Rose's worst decision? Why?
4. Given what you know about the background of Rose and other immigrants to America in the early 1900s, do you think you could have succeeded as an immigrant? Explain your answer.

Read and Respond: *Hope in My Heart*

Hope in My Heart: Sophia's Immigrant Diary is a very realistic fictional account of one nine-year-old Italian immigrant's experience in crossing the Atlantic Ocean in the steerage section of a ship and then entering Ellis Island hoping to become an American.

Note: Sophia's story is continued in *Home at Last: Sophia's Immigrant Diary.*

Assignment

1. Read *Hope in My Heart: Sophia's Immigrant Diary* by Kathryn Lasky.

2. Answer the questions below, and share your responses in a small group or class discussion.

Comprehension Questions

1. Which person is sick to her stomach most of the time on the ship?

2. Why is Sophia put in quarantine at Ellis Island?

3. Who is Rafi?

4. Who does Sophia help while in quarantine?

5. What country is Maureen from?

6. Which people help Sophia and Maureen get out of quarantine?

Discussion Starters

1. How does Rafi educate and help Sophia?

2. What disadvantages does Sophia have in struggling to join her parents—in language and understanding?

3. What advantages in terms of character, personality, and intelligence does Sophia possess?

4. What do the inspectors at Ellis Island think is wrong with Maureen? Why do they think that?

5. How are immigrants mistreated at Ellis Island? Who do you think is responsible?

6. What would happen to Sophia if she went back home alone?

7. Should her parents have gone back to Italy when Sophia couldn't leave with them?

8. Why did people come to America even if they were sick like Mr. Joe?

Making It Personal

1. How would you feel if you were Sophia? What emotions would you have?

2. Which character did you like or admire most? Give several reasons.

3. What did you think was the saddest event? Why?

4. Do you have any living relatives who immigrated to America? When did they come, and where did they enter?

Immigrant Diaries

Assignment

Read one of the fictional diaries described on the next page or one of the many other fictional diaries in the *Dear America*, *My America*, *American Diaries*, and other diary series. Share your observations with your classmates.

Immigrant Diary Notes

Title of Diary: _____

Author: _____

Immigrant's Personal Data

Name, age, gender: _____

Native country & culture: _____

Personality: _____

Character traits: _____

Hopes & dreams: _____

Setting

Historical time period: _____

Immigrant's destination: _____

Problems & conflicts: _____

_____

Other Major Characters

Family members: _____

Friends: _____

Miscellaneous

Resolution (the end): _____

Impressions (your personal thoughts about the main character): _____

_____

Questions (things you didn't understand): _____

_____

Leading the Discussion

Write three discussion questions to ask the group about the diary you read. The questions could center around the motivation of the characters and what readers think about the judgment of the main characters.

  1. _____

  2. _____

  3. _____

| 1600 | 1650 | 1700 | 1750 | 1800 | 1850 | 1900 | 1950 | 2000 |

Immigrant Diaries *(cont.)*

Bartoletti, Susan Campbell. *The Journal of Finn Reardon: A Newsie*. My Name Is America Series. New York: Scholastic, 2003.

This is a riveting story about an immigrant boy in New York who gets involved in the 1899 newsboy strike for fairer treatment by the big newspapers.

Denenberg, Barry. *So Far from Home: The Diary of Mary Driscoll, an Irish Mill Girl*. Dear America Series. New York: Scholastic, 1997.

This is an outstanding story of a thirteen-year-old girl's journey from Ireland during the great potato famine of 1847 and her experiences in the Massachusetts clothing mills.

Durbin, William. *The Journal of Otto Peltonen: A Finnish Immigrant*. My Name Is America Series. New York: Scholastic, 2003.

This is a powerful story of a young immigrant boy's journey from Finland to Minnesota, where he becomes an iron miner involved in an effort to form a union for better working conditions.

Lasky, Kathryn. *Home at Last: Sophia's Immigrant Diary*. My America Series. New York: Scholastic, 2003.

This is the story of an Italian immigrant girl's experiences adjusting to American life in Boston, Massachusetts. It is the sequel to *Hope in My Heart*.

—————. *Dreams in the Golden Country: The Diary of Zipporah Feldman, a Jewish Immigrant Girl*. Dear America Series. New York: Scholastic, 1998.

This is a gripping story of a stubborn and intelligent Russian Jewish immigrant girl living in New York in 1903.

—————. *A Journey to the New World: The Diary of Remember Patience Whipple*. Dear America Series. New York: Scholastic, 1996.

This is the story of a Pilgrim girl on the Mayflower traveling to and arriving at Plymouth Settlement in 1620. The suffering on the voyage across the Atlantic and the experiences of the Pilgrims in a new land are seen from a young girl's point of view.

White, Ellen Emerson. *Voyage on the Great* Titanic: *The Diary of Margaret Ann Brady*. Dear America Series. New York: Scholastic, 1998.

This is the story of an orphan Irish immigrant girl's adventures on the *Titanic*'s voyage to America.

Yep, Laurence. *The Journal of Wong Ming-Chung: A Chinese Miner*. My Name Is America Series. New York: Scholastic, 2000.

This is the story of one Chinese immigrant's voyage to America and his experiences in the California Gold Rush.

Create Your Own Diary

Assignment

1. Start your own diary or journal—today. Don't put it off. Imagine that your children will someday read your diary, that it might be found by a researcher in the distant future, or even that you may find this diary when you are an adult.

2. Record at least one entry each day, even if it is short and doesn't seem too important now.

3. Describe the important events that are going on in your personal life.

4. Record some of your daily habits and personal feelings about life.

5. Mention events in the world or your community that are affecting your life or may affect your life in the future.

6. Describe books you are reading that influence your thinking.

7. Mention your dreams, aspirations, and hopes for the future.

8. Describe important people in your life, such as parents and teachers, and tell how they influence you.

9. Reflect on the meaning of life.

Hints for Success

- Be honest with yourself.
- Express your deepest thoughts.
- Feel free to change your mind about people and events.
- Enjoy the creative experience.
- Don't quit.

Getting Started

Day One

Events: _____

_____

Feelings and Emotions: _____

_____

Reflections: _____

_____

Day Two

Events: _____

_____

Feelings and Emotions: _____

_____

Reflections: _____

_____

Readers' Theater Notes

Behind the Scenes

Readers' Theater is drama that does not require costumes, props, a stage, or memorization. It is done in the classroom by groups of students who become the cast of the dramatic reading.

Staging

Place seven stools or chairs in a semicircle at the front of your class or in a separate staging area. Generally, no costumes are used in this type of dramatization, but students dressed in similar clothing or colors can have a nice effect. Simple props can be used but are not required.

Scripting

Each member of your group should have a clearly marked script. Performers should practice several times before presenting the play to the class.

Performing

Performers should enter the classroom quietly and seriously. They should sit silently without moving and wait with their heads lowered. The first reader should begin, and the other readers should focus on whomever is reading, except when they are performing.

Assignment

Read the Readers' Theater script chosen by your teacher about Albert Einstein. Work with your assigned group to prepare for your performance, and share your interpretation of the script with your class.

Extensions

Write your own Readers' Theater script based on one of the following events or another topic related to your study of the American immigrant experience. Practice your script with a group of classmates, and then perform it for the rest of the class.

- An immigrant is held at Ellis Island because she has a disease.

- A young Chinese girl waits at Angel Island for permission to enter the country.

- A young Italian boy tries to find work to help feed his family.

- A child your age has just entered your school, but he speaks another language and does not know any English.

- A child is aboard a ship in the steerage section. Describe the voyage from the child's point of view.

- An immigrant is traveling to America aboard the *Titanic* in the steerage section. Describe the catastrophe.

Background Information:
Albert Einstein

Albert Einstein was born in Ulm, Germany, in 1879. He rarely spoke as a toddler, often had a bad temper, and was sometimes mean to his sister. Albert loved gadgets, especially a compass given to him by his father when he was four. He liked to build houses from cards. He once built one fourteen stories tall. In school, he only studied what interested him, which included science and Latin. He liked math, but he hated memorizing anything, and he often failed to pay attention because he was usually daydreaming. He liked playing the violin anywhere, including in the park. He was often the brunt of jokes by his classmates because of his Jewish race (he was often the only Jew in his class), his tendency to daydream, or his need to constantly ask questions. They called him "Biedermeier," a word meaning something like "nerd."

Einstein did not get accepted to the Swiss Institute of Technology immediately following high school. In fact, he had to study for a year more before he finally got accepted. Even in college, he was bored, often skipped classes, and failed to pay attention to instructions, once resulting in one of his experiments blowing up. Despite his academic difficulties, Einstein got a job that he enjoyed at a patent office in Switzerland. He began serious work on physics concepts and published four of his most important papers in 1905. One dealt with the idea of atoms and molecules and their movement. Another paper argued that light traveled as both a particle and a wave, a very radical idea for its time. His paper on "The Special Theory of Relativity" would radically change ideas of time and space in the world of physics. Experiments in 1919 during a solar eclipse confirmed his theory. In 1922, he won the Nobel Prize in Physics for his work on the nature of light.

As a Jewish scientist, he recognized the danger to his own life and his family posed by the rise to absolute power of Adolph Hitler and the Nazi regime, which controlled Germany. Einstein also realized the potential threat to all Europe and to world peace by the German military machine. Hitler's anti-semitism (anti-Jewish hatred and fears) encouraged many Jews to emigrate from Germany. In 1933, Nazis ransacked Einstein's property in Germany. Einstein renounced his German citizenship and accepted a position the same year at Princeton University at a new science center for advanced studies. In 1939, he wrote a letter to President Franklin Roosevelt explaining the possible threat to the world if the Nazis managed to build an atomic bomb. This letter helped the president understand the danger and eventually led to efforts in the United States to create the atomic bomb. In 1940, Einstein became a U.S. citizen. He died at Princeton in 1955 at the age of seventy-six. Einstein is one of the best-known immigrants to the United States.

Readers' Theater:
Relativity! Relativity! Relativity!

This script imagines Albert Einstein in a class as a young man thinking about his famous concept of relativity. There are seven speaking parts:

> Narrator   Second Student
> Professor   Third Student
> Einstein   Friend
> First Student

Narrator: We are peeking into a lecture hall located in a college in Switzerland. The students are listening to a professor speak. Young Albert Einstein is there with a violin under his arm staring dreamily into space.

Professor: So the speed of light is the fastest thing in the universe. Nothing else can travel as fast. And you, Albert, are you awake? What do you think of this principle of physics? Or are you too tired from playing the violin for pigeons in the park to listen to your teachers?

Einstein: (Answering rather dreamily)
I think it's all relative.

Professor: Einstein, you will never amount to anything. You waste your time reading unimportant essays, playing the violin like a roving beggar, and dreaming nonsense!

Einstein: But, you see,
$E=mc^2$
$E=mc^2$ because it's all relative.
Light is relative.
Time is relative.
Space is relative.
Motion is relative.
Because . . .
Energy equals mass
times the speed of light
times the speed of light again.

Professor: Nonsense! Rubbish! Dunderhead! You need to listen to your teachers and learn.

First Student: But what does it mean?

Second Student: It means Albert's been dreaming again.

Readers' Theater:
Relativity! Relativity! Relativity! *(cont.)*

Professor: It means he hasn't been paying attention!

Third Student: He's a "Biedermeier," a brain in math and science, but he can't do anything useful. Albert hasn't even learned to drive a car. He still rides his bike or walks. He will never be successful in life.

Professor: You are a very clever boy, Einstein, an extremely clever boy, but you have one great fault: you never let yourself be told anything. Your experiment in the lab exploded yesterday because you didn't listen to your teacher.

Einstein: It was just a slight miscalculation, but it was very interesting.

First Student: It was certainly interesting. The blast nearly destroyed the lab and burned his hand.

Friend: Albert is totally brilliant, but he is also completely absentminded. He sometimes forgets where he lives and just keeps walking or riding his bike until he remembers where he is going.

Einstein: (As if he never heard the interruptions)
So, you see,
$E=mc^2$
$E=mc^2$ because it's all relative.
Energy equals mass
times the speed of light
times the speed of light again.
It's the theory . . .
of relativity.

All Students: Relativity . . . relativity . . . relativity . . .
That's all Albert ever thinks about.

Narrator: Albert was absentminded, but he was also brilliant. He hated listening to his teachers and often did forget where he was going or even where he lived. Einstein did eventually become famous for his theory of relativity and his work on the nature of light. He said that anyone who has never made a mistake has never tried anything new.

Teacher Lesson Plans for Social Studies

Patriotic Art and Anthems

Objective: Students will recognize the significance of the Statue of Liberty and certain patriotic practices in American history.

Materials: copies of The Statue of Liberty (pages 68–70) and Patriotic Practices (page 71); rulers, poster board or construction paper, green tissue paper or paint, glue; additional books, encyclopedias, and Internet sources for enrichment

Procedure

1. Review the information on The Statue of Liberty. Explain the assignment on page 69 for building a 3-D model of the statue. Alternatively, you may wish to have students draw a 2-D model of the statue. Explain the idea of scale measurements. Provide materials for building or drawing the models.

2. Review the poem on page 70 and review the meanings of the terms used in "The New Colossus." Have students practice the poem alone, in pairs, or as a class. Then recite the poem as a class.

3. Have students study the "Pledge of Allegiance," as well as the notes underneath the pledge. Have them practice the pledge alone, in pairs, or as a class. Then recite the pledge as a class.

4. Have students study the first verse of the "Star-Spangled Banner," as well as its history. Recite or sing the anthem as a class.

Assessment: Assess the statue by the degree of detail and use of scale. Assess the poems on oral presentations.

Timelines, Maps, and Numbers

Objectives: Students will learn to derive information from a timeline and maps and compute percentages.

Materials: copies of Immigration Timeline (pages 72–73), World Map: Sources of Immigrants (page 74), Working with Facts and Figures (pages 75–76), and American Roots (page 77); calculators and atlases; additional books, encyclopedias, texts, almanacs, and Internet sources for enrichment

Procedure

1. Collect available resources so that students have plenty of materials from which to find information.

2. Review the concept of a timeline using the school year as an example.

3. Reproduce and distribute Immigration Timeline. Review the various events listed on the timeline. Instruct students to place additional dates on the timeline as described in the assignment on page 73. Students may want to use the readings from the beginning of the book to locate the ten extra dates for their timelines.

4. Reproduce and review with students the World Map: Sources of Immigrants. Help students identify and label the countries with the use of an atlas.

5. Reproduce Working with Facts and Figures and American Roots. Remind students how to compute percentages. Have students do calculations by hand or with a calculator.

Assessment: Verify the accuracy of the dates and events that students added to the timeline. Verify and correct the world map. Check the accuracy of calculations on the three math pages.

Teacher Lesson Plans for Social Studies *(cont.)*

Immigrant Biographies and Heritage

Objectives: Students will develop skills in finding, organizing, and presenting biographical and research information.

Materials: copies of Immigrant Biographies (pages 78–80), Who Are You? Writing Your Autobiography (pages 81–82), and Discovering Your Immigrant Heritage (pages 83–85); additional books, encyclopedias, and Internet sources for enrichment

Procedure

1. Have students use the suggested biographies or other sources to select a subject to research. Students should complete the biographical description and outline on page 78. Students should then use the evaluation and questioning guide on page 79 to understand their subjects. Encourage students to share their ideas and concerns with other students in small-group or whole-class discussions.

2. Encourage students to create their own autobiography using Who Are You? Writing Your Autobiography. Encourage students to assess their goals and future opportunities and reflect on the legacy they want to leave for their children and the world.

3. Reproduce Discovering Your Immigrant Heritage. Encourage students to use their research skills to conduct interviews with relatives familiar with their personal heritage. Help students evaluate their research experience and appreciate their unique cultural heritage.

Assessment: Assess students on their oral classroom presentations, as well as their written work. Stress the importance of evaluating and understanding their cultural linkage with all Americans.

John Muir and National Parks

Objectives: Students will learn to appreciate the contributions of immigrant John Muir and the importance of national parks.

Materials: copies of John Muir and National Parks (pages 86–89); additional almanacs, encyclopedias, books about national parks, and Internet sources

Procedure

1. Reproduce John Muir and National Parks. Review facts about John Muir, and direct children in finding sources about national parks. Consider showing part of Ken Burns's special film history of national parks. Have students research the national parks listed on pages 86–88.

2. Help students use the map on page 89 to locate some of the U.S. national parks.

Assessment: Assess students on the accuracy of their information about the listed parks and their locations on the map.

The Statue of Liberty

The Statue of Liberty was a gift from France presented to the United States on July 4, 1884. It was a symbol recognizing the long friendship between France and the United States, which began in the Revolutionary War. It was also a centennial gift from France to the United States celebrating the 100 years of the United States as a nation and the commitment to liberty of both nations. Because of its location on Liberty Island, the Statue of Liberty also became a symbol of America's welcoming embrace to the immigrants of the world.

The Statue of Liberty was created by a French sculptor, Frederic Auguste Bartholdi, who took twelve years to finish the monument. The face was based on the sculptor's mother's face when she was a young woman. Completed in 1884, the statue remained on display in France for a year before it was dismantled in 1885 and sent to New York in 214 huge packing crates.

The statue was then reassembled on a granite pedestal built on a twelve-acre island on what is now known as Liberty Island. The official name of the statue is *Liberty Enlightening the World*. It was dedicated with great fanfare by President Grover Cleveland on October 28, 1886. The statue weighs 225 tons and is covered with copper sheeting that weighs 200,000 pounds (100 tons). There are 167 steps from the bottom of the pedestal to the top of the pedestal and 168 steps from the bottom of the statue to the head. There are 54 rungs on the ladder leading to the arm holding the torch.

People Who Drove the Project

A number of people were involved in getting the project done. Edouard de Laboulaye, a French professor of law, suggested the idea of a statue to French sculptor Frederic Auguste Bartholdi in 1865. Bartholdi went to America in 1871 and proposed the idea to important Americans, including President Grant, but he could get no financial support. He began work anyway, counting on French support. Gustave Eiffel, the structural engineer who designed the Eiffel Tower in Paris, designed and supervised the statue's internal framework. Joseph Pulitzer, a New York newspaper publisher and immigrant to America, led a campaign to raise money in America to build the pedestal and finish the statue's construction in America. Emma Lazarus, a Jewish immigrant poet, wrote a sonnet, a type of poem, called "The New Colossus" for the pedestal fund. The last part of the poem was engraved on the pedestal in 1903.

The Statue of Liberty *(cont.)*

Assignment

1. Form a small group of four to six students. You are now a team of builders that will construct a 3-D model of the Statue of Liberty using poster board or construction paper. Alternatively, you can draw a 2-D model on paper.

2. To make your model an accurate replica, convert the measurements in feet below to centimeters with 1 foot equal to about $\frac{1}{2}$ centimeter. (You must first round the statue facts to the nearest whole foot.) Round up your answer to the next centimeter, if needed. Your model will be about 30 inches high.

3. Assign different parts of the statue to team members.

4. Use green tissue paper or paint to decorate the statue.

5. Once your team has completed the statue, construct or draw the pedestal and foundation using the same scale.

Statue Facts	Model Measurements (approximate)
Weight: 450,000 pounds or 225 tons	
Height (from base to torch tip): 151 ft. 1 in.	_76_ cm
Height (from foundation of pedestal to torch tip): 305 ft. 1 in.	_____ cm
Height (from heel to top of head): 111 ft. 1 in.	_____ cm
Number of steps from land level to top of pedestal: 167	
Number of steps inside statue to the head: 168	
Number of rungs on the ladder leading to torch arm: 54	
Hand length: 16 ft. 5 in.	_____ cm
Length of index finger: 8 ft.	_____ cm
Thickness of head (ear to ear): 10 ft.	_____ cm
Length of nose: 4 ft. 6 in.	_____ cm
Length of right arm: 42 ft.	_____ cm
Width of mouth: 3 ft.	_____ cm
Width of tablet: 13 ft. 7 in.	_____ cm
Length of tablet: 23 ft. 7 in.	_____ cm
Thickness of tablet: 2 ft.	_____ cm
Height of granite pedestal: 89 ft.	_____ cm
Height of concrete foundation: 65 ft.	_____ cm

The Statue of Liberty *(cont.)*

This poem, by immigrant Emma Lazarus, is engraved on the pedestal below the statue. It is a welcome to immigrants and a tribute to their contributions to America.

> **The New Colossus**
> Not like the brazen giant of Greek fame, 1
> With conquering limbs astride from land to land; 2
> Here at our sea-washed, sunset gates shall stand 3
> A mighty woman with a torch, whose flame 4
> Is the imprisoned lightning, and her name 5
> Mother of Exiles. From her beacon-hand 6
> Glows world-wide welcome, her mild eyes command 7
> The air-bridged harbor that twin cities frame. 8
> "Keep, ancient lands, your storied pomp!" cries she, 9
> With silent lips. "Give me your tired, your poor, 10
> Your huddled masses yearning to breathe free, 11
> The wretched refuse of your teeming shore; 12
> Send these, the homeless, tempest-tost to me, 13
> I lift my lamp beside the golden door!" 14

Understanding Poetry

Directions: Like many poems, "The New Colossus" refers to earlier events or objects and uses very expressive, figurative language. Read the explanations and references listed below as you study the poem.

Lines 1 and 2: The statue is not like the *Colossus of Rhodes*, an ancient statue that stood in the harbor of a port with each leg on points of land sticking into the harbor as a symbol of power and wealth.

Line 3: *sea-washed, sunset gates*—The journey to America has ended at this welcoming statue and harbor.

Line 4: *A mighty woman with a torch*—Lady Liberty

Lines 4 and 5: *whose flame is the imprisoned lightning*—The torch is a symbol of controlled power (lightning), light (symbol of hope), and welcoming from the nation.

Lines 5 and 6: *her name Mother of Exiles*—The United States is a welcoming mother to exiles, or people displaced from their own countries for many reasons.

Lines 6 and 7: *beacon-hand glows world-wide welcome*—The lighted torch is a symbol of welcome.

Line 8: *air-bridged harbor*—Air is the only cover for the harbor between two cities.

Line 9: *"Keep, ancient lands, your storied pomp!"*—The old worlds of Europe and Asia can keep their traditions and ancient practices.

Line 11: *huddled masses yearning to breathe free*—large numbers of poor people huddled together seeking freedom and opportunity

Line 12: *wretched refuse of your teeming shore*—the many poor and unwanted people waiting to get away from the old countries

Line 13: *homeless, tempest-tost*—people without a home who have endured a stormy, dangerous journey to freedom

Line 14: *I lift my lamp beside the golden door!*—The statue and lamp will guide the travelers to opportunity and freedom.

Patriotic Practices

The New Colossus

Assignment

1. Study "The New Colossus" and the notes below the poem on page 70.
2. Practice saying the poem alone, with a friend, or with the class.
3. Recite the poem as a class.

Pledge of Allegiance

Assignment

1. Study the "Pledge of Allegiance" and the notes underneath the pledge below.
2. Practice saying the pledge alone, with a friend, or with the class.
3. Recite the pledge as a class.

Pledge of Allegiance

I pledge allegiance to the flag of the United States of America and to the republic for which it stands, one nation under God, indivisible, with liberty and justice for all.

The pledge was first written for a youth magazine in the 1890s as a way of expressing a common faith and loyalty to the nation. With a few changes, it became a common practice to recite the pledge as a group before official government meetings, such as city council and school board meetings.

Meaning

allegiance—loyalty
republic—a nation of free people governed by fair, just, and equal laws with leaders elected by the people
one nation—there are many states and people but all are one
indivisible—can't be broken apart or separated
with liberty and justice for all—all people in the country are entitled to freedom and fair treatment

The Star-Spangled Banner

Assignment

1. Study the lines of "The Star-Spangled Banner" below.
2. Read the history of "The Star-Spangled Banner."
3. Recite or sing the anthem as a class.

The Star-Spangled Banner

O say can you see, by the dawn's early light,
What so proudly we hail'd at the twilight's last gleaming?
Whose broad stripes and bright stars through the perilous fight
O'er the ramparts we watch'd were so gallantly streaming?
And the rocket's red glare, the bombs bursting in air,
Gave proof through the night that our flag was still there,
O say does that star-spangled banner yet wave
O'er the land of the free and the home of the brave?

"The Star-Spangled Banner" became the official national anthem in 1931 as a symbol of national unity. Francis Scott Key wrote it as a poem on the back of an envelope in 1814 as he observed the shelling of Fort McHenry in Baltimore by the British during the War of 1812. Key was on the British warship to negotiate the release of an American doctor held by the British. The tattered flag's survival symbolized the survival of the fort and the nation.

1600	1650	1700	1750	1800	1850	1900	1950	2000

Immigration Timeline

1607–1776—The first wave of immigrants settles in America.

1607—English settlers land in Chesapeake Bay, Virginia, to found the colony of Jamestown.

1619—The first black indentured servants arrive in Jamestown.

—African slaves arrive soon after.

1784—German immigrant John Jacob Astor arrives in Maryland to start his fur company and his fortune.

1790—The Naturalization Act grants citizenship to "free whites" who have lived in the country for two years.

— The U.S. population is nearly four million.

1820–1870—A second wave of immigration brings about 7,500,000 immigrants, largely from Ireland and Germany.

1845—The Great Potato Famine occurs in Ireland leading to massive migration to America.

1849—The California Gold Rush encourages immigration to California from many countries.

1851—An estimated 55,000 Chinese immigrants are working in the California gold fields and in other states.

1855—Castle Garden, the first immigration station in the United States, opens in New York City.

1869—The first transcontinental railroad in America is completed with the help of thousands of Chinese laborers.

1870—A new naturalization law restricts citizenship to those of European or African descent.

1876—Scottish immigrant Alexander Graham Bell invents the telephone.

1881–1920—A third wave of immigrants brings 23,500,000 immigrants to the United States, mainly from southern and eastern Europe.

1881—The assassination of Russian Czar Alexander II leads to pogroms against Jews, causing many Jewish families to immigrate to America.

1882—The Chinese Exclusion Act prohibits the immigration of Chinese to the United States.

1883—Emma Lazarus writes the poem "The New Colossus" for the Statue of Liberty.

1886—The Statue of Liberty is formally dedicated in New York City.

1890—Jane Addams establishes Hull House in Chicago to help immigrants and other urban poor.

—The U.S. census counts only 325,000 American Indians, down from an estimated ten million in 1600.

1891—The first U.S. Bureau of Immigration is established.

1892—The federal immigration center on Ellis Island opens. Annie Moore is the first immigrant to be processed.

1897—Fire destroys many buildings on Ellis Island.

1900—The U.S. census records seventy-six million people in the country.

1907—Ellis Island experiences the highest rate of immigration with over one million immigrants.

—Japanese laborers are allowed to immigrate to Hawaii but not the U.S. mainland.

1600   1650   1700   1750   1800   1850   1900   1950   2000

Immigration Timeline (cont.)

1910—Angel Island Immigration Center, called "The Guardian of the Western Gate," is opened near San Francisco.

1918—Quota systems are enacted to favor British and Western European immigration.

1924—The Immigration Act of 1924 drastically reduces legal immigration into the United States.

1929–1940—The Great Depression halts immigration to the U.S., and some immigrants leave.

1935—Writer Isaac Bashevis Singer immigrates to the U.S. from Poland.
—Architect I. M. Pei immigrates to the U.S. from China.

1939—Austrian immigrant Felix Frankfurter becomes Associate Justice of the U.S. Supreme Court.

1940—A fire destroys a main building at Angel Island, and the center is closed.

1942—Italian immigrant Enrico Fermi directs experiments that lead to the first controlled nuclear chain reaction.

1943—The Chinese Exclusion Act is repealed.

1948—About 400,000 war refugees from Europe are admitted into the U.S.

1952—A new law changes the quota system of immigrants.
—Hungarian immigrant Edward Teller leads the development of the hydrogen bomb.

1954—The immigration center at Ellis Island is closed.

1959—More than 200,000 Cubans flee revolution in Cuba to the U.S.; most Cubans settle in Florida.

1965 to the Present—A fourth wave of immigrants brings people from Mexico, Central America, and many Asian countries.

1965—A new immigration quota system is passed.

1975—More than 130,000 Vietnamese flee to America following the U.S. withdrawal from South Vietnam.

1980—The Refugee Act allows ten million immigrants to be granted legal citizenship.

1986—The renovations are finished on the Statue of Liberty.
—Amnesty is granted to 2.7 million illegal immigrants.

1990—Ellis Island reopens as a museum dedicated to the history of immigration.

2000—The U.S. Census records the population at more than 260 million.

2009—Barack Obama, son of an immigrant, is elected president of the United States.

Assignment

- Find at least ten dates in American history to add to the timeline. These dates could include wars, inventions, presidential elections, disasters, or sporting events, among other events.
- Create a visual timeline with these facts on a roll of white paper, such as shelf paper, rolled computer paper, or small adding machine rolls.
- Block off squares or rectangles with a ruler.
- Write the date and the event at the top of each square.
- Draw a picture to illustrate each event in the lower half of each square. Use books and other sources to help you.
- Use colored pencils or thin line markers to color each event.

1600 1650 1700 1750 1800 1850 1900 1950 2000

World Map: Sources of Immigrants

Immigrants came from almost every country in the world. Some came in huge numbers because of famine or revolution. Others came to improve their lives and for better jobs.

Directions: Using the world map shown below, number the countries where immigrants came from. The countries are listed and numbered below. Use an atlas to help you find countries that you are unsure of.

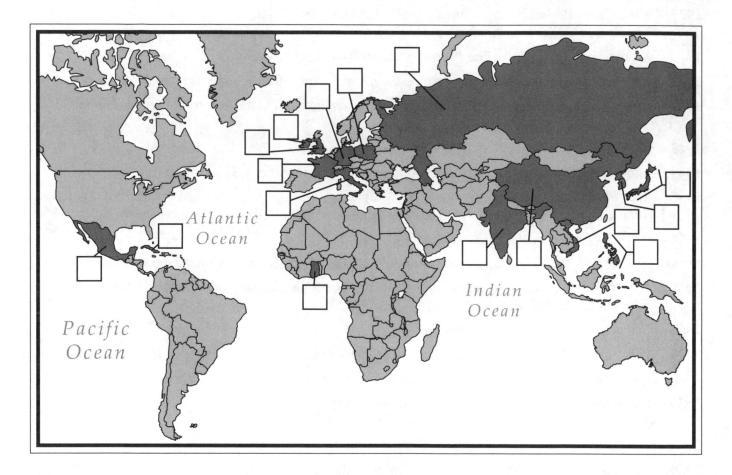

Countries from which immigrants have come:

1. Germany
2. Ireland
3. England
4. Mexico

5. Italy
6. Russia
7. Poland
8. France

9. Ghana, formerly The Gold Coast
10. Cuba
11. China
12. Korea

13. Japan
14. The Philippines
15. India
16. Vietnam

#3147 A Nation of Immigrants   74   *©Teacher Created Resources*

Working with Facts and Figures

Directions: Use your knowledge of charts and percentages to find the approximate number of people who immigrated to the United States from each country or area in the 100 years between 1820 and 1920. The total number of immigrants was 30,000,000.

Note: Percentage is determined by multiplication.

Example: 7% = 0.07

$$\begin{array}{r} 30,000,000 \\ \times\ 0.07 \\ \hline 2,100,000 \end{array}$$

Place	Percentage
Italy and Southern Europe	15.5%
Scandanavian Countries (Norway/Sweden)	6%
Canada and Latin American Countries	10%
Great Britain	11%
Poland and Central European Countries	13%
Russia and Eastern European Countries	10%
Germany	16%
Ireland	12%
Other European Countries	3%
African Countries	1%

Place	Number of Immigrants
1. Italy and Southern Europe	_____
2. Scandinavian Countries (Norway/Sweden)	_____
3. Canada and Latin American Countries	_____
4. Great Britain	_____
5. Poland and Central European Countries	_____
6. Russia and Eastern European Countries	_____
7. Germany	_____
8. Ireland	_____
9. Other European Countries	_____
10. African Countries	_____

1600   1650   1700   1750   1800   1850   1900   1950   2000

Working with Facts and Figures *(cont.)*

Directions: Use your knowledge of math to find the solutions to these problems related to immigration.

1. It took almost four months for passengers to get to America from Europe in the middle 1700s. By 1840, it took about fifteen days. About how many days shorter was the trip by 1840?

   _____

2. There are about 300 million Americans. About 100 million can trace their ancestry to a relative who passed through Ellis Island in its history from 1892 to 1954. What percentage of the population can trace their ancestry to immigrants coming through Ellis Island?

   _____

3. More than one million immigrants passed through Ellis Island in 1907, its peak year of use. A total of fifteen million immigrants entered the U.S. through Ellis Island altogether. What percentage of the total entered in 1907?

   _____

4. What was the average number of immigrants entering the U.S. daily through Ellis Island in 1907?

   _____

5. In the early 1800s, more than one half of the passengers were ill on the voyage to America. Additionally, one tenth of the passengers died en route.

   For every million passengers, how many were sick on the voyage? _____

   For every million passengers, how many died on the voyage? _____

6. New York City became home to more immigrants than any other city. By 1700, at least eighteen languages were spoken in the city. Today, at least 100 languages are represented in the immigrant communities. How many more languages are spoken today in New York City?

   _____

7. By the 1900s, at least three quarters of each of the large cities—New York, Boston, Chicago, Cleveland, and Detroit—were populated by immigrants. What percentage of each of these cities was populated by immigrants?

   _____

8. About 200,000 to 300,000 immigrants were turned back from Ellis Island in its sixty-two year history, but about seventy-nine out of every eighty immigrants were accepted. What percentage of immigrants was accepted?

   _____

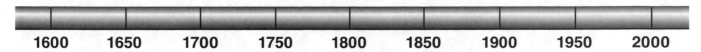

American Roots

Because the United States is a nation of immigrants, all Americans can trace their roots to other nations or to the American Indians, who came here millions of years ago.

Directions: Use the chart below to help compute the number of Americans who can claim ancestry for each group. Many people, of course, claim ancestry in two or more groups. For this activity, the U.S. population (rounded to the nearest million) is 303,000,000.

Example: 303,000,000 x 12.5% = 37,875,000

$$
\begin{array}{r}
303{,}000{,}000 \\
\times \quad 0.125 \\
\hline
37{,}875{,}000
\end{array}
$$

Percent of Population Claiming Ancestry		Number of People Claiming Ancestry
Germany	14.5%	_____
Africa	12%	_____
Ireland	10%	_____
England	8%	_____
Mexico	6.9%	_____
Italy	5.2%	_____
Poland	3%	_____
France	2.7%	_____
Scotland	1.6%	_____
Holland	1.5%	_____

Directions: Compute these percentages of the population.

American Indian	1%	_____
Native Hawaiian/Pacific Islander	0.2%	_____
Asian	4.4%	_____
Black	12.8%	_____
Hispanic/Latino	15.1%	_____
White (not Hispanic)	80.1%	_____
Foreign-born	12.1%	_____

Directions: Compute these percentages of the population.

Under twenty-one years of age	24.5%	_____
Over sixty-five years of age	12.6%	_____
Over eighty-five years of age	1.8%	_____

| 1600 | 1650 | 1700 | 1750 | 1800 | 1850 | 1900 | 1950 | 2000 |

Immigrant Biographies

A biography tells about the life of a person. There are many biographies written about the lives of immigrants who have influenced American history and the children of immigrants who grew up in immigrant families.

Assignment

Read one biography about an important American immigrant or a child who grew up in an immigrant family and succeeded in some way. You can choose one listed on page 80 or select another biography from the library about an immigrant that appeals to you.

Describe four experiences that were unique to the person you read about because he or she was an immigrant or the child of immigrants. Use the questions on page 79 to help you with your description.

Special Experiences as an Immigrant or a Child of Immigrants

1. _____
   _____

2. _____
   _____

3. _____
   _____

4. _____
   _____

Directions: Create a biographical outline of the person's life by listing eight important events that occurred in his or her life. These might include special events in childhood and teen years, educational opportunities, or ideas and dreams.

Biographical Outline of Important Events

1. _____
2. _____
3. _____
4. _____
5. _____
6. _____
7. _____
8. _____

Immigrant Biographies (cont.)

Directions: Use these questions to help you understand the importance of your person, as well as obstacles he or she had to overcome.

Questioning the Subject

1. What important accomplishments did your subject achieve? What did he or she do that was important for his or her family, culture, country, or the world?

2. How did the experiences of the person's youth affect his or her adult life?

3. Why did this person or this person's family leave home and immigrate to America?

4. What leadership qualities did the subject demonstrate?

5. How did your subject demonstrate courage and tenacity (an unwillingness to quit)?

6. What other character traits did your subject have that you admired? How did he or she demonstrate those traits?

7. Would you have liked to know this person? Why?

8. What was the greatest challenge your subject faced?

9. What was the saddest event in the life of the person?

10. What lessons can you learn about life from the person you read about?

Questioning History

- What historical events, laws, or beliefs did you not completely understand while reading about the subject of your biography?

- How has the world changed since the lifetime of the person you read about?

- What changes of attitude have occurred in America since your subject was young? (These attitudes could relate to racial stereotypes [beliefs about certain people], opinions about different religions, and prejudices about cultures and languages.)

- Why have many people become less prejudiced about people who come from other countries and cultures?

- What events or actions sometimes cause people today to resent immigrants and people of different cultures?

- What modern inventions help people see the humanity in others and appreciate their needs?

- How did your subject help other people recognize the virtues (the good things) about his or her culture?

Sharing a Life

Use the notes you took and your evaluation of your biographical subject to share information with your class or a group. Use the questions on both pages to increase your understanding of immigration and history.

Immigrant Biographies (cont.)

Biographies of Immigrants

Delano, Marfe Ferguson. *Genius: A Photobiography of Albert Einstein.* Washington, DC: National Geographic, 2005.
This is an enjoyable biography with many pictures of Einstein's life.

Haven, Kendall F. *Alexander Graham Bell: Inventor and Visionary.* New York: Franklin Watts, 2003.
This is an easy-to-read record of the Scottish immigrant inventor's life and work.

Lasky, Kathryn. *John Muir: America's First Environmentalist.* Cambridge: Candlewick Press, 2006.
This is a superbly illustrated story of John Muir's travels and accomplishments.

Lassieur, Allison. *Albert Einstein: Genius of the Twentieth Century.* New York: Franklin Watts, 2005.
This is an excellent, detailed account of the scientist's life and work.

Krull, Kathleen. *Houdini: World's Greatest Mystery Man and Escape King.* New York: Walker, 2005.
This is a very clever, well-illustrated, easy-to read story of the Hungarian immigrant.

McLendon, Jacquelyn. *Phillis Wheatley: A Revolutionary Poet.* New York: Rosen, 2003.
This is a superior account of the poet's life and times as an immigrant slave.

Murphy, Jim. *Pick & Shovel Poet: The Journeys of Pascal D'Angelo.* New York: Clarion, 2000.
Masterfully written, this is the story of an extraordinary Italian immigrant who did hard manual labor digging roads and railways. He recorded his feelings and faith in his own book called *Son of Italy*.

Stalcup, Ann. *Leo Politi: Artist of the Angels.* New York: Silver Moon Press, 2004.
This children's artist's Italian immigrant parents returned to Italy when he was a small child. He reimmigrated to America when he was twenty-one years old.

Weidt, Maryann N. *Mr. Blue Jeans: A Story About Levi Strauss.* Minneapolis: Carolrholda Books, 1990.
This is an interesting biography of the German Jewish immigrant who invented jeans.

Biographies of the Children of Immigrants

Giblin, James Cross. *Charles A. Lindbergh: A Human Hero.* New York: Clarion, 1997.
This is a detailed and well-written story of the great aviator whose grandfather and father emigrated from Sweden.

Marcovitz, Hal. *Cesar Chavez.* New York: Chelsea House, 2003.
This is the story of the labor union organizer's life as a child of immigrants.

Partridge, Elizabeth. *Restless Spirit: The Life and Work of Dorothea Lange.* New York: Viking, 1998.
This is an interesting story of the famed photographer of the poor during the Great Depression. She was the granddaughter of immigrants who helped raise her.

Shichtman, Sandra H. *Colin Powell.* Berkeley Heights, NJ: Enslow, 2005.
This is the story of Colin Powell's career. He is the son of Jamaican immigrants.

Zuehlke, Jeffrey. *Henry Ford.* Minneapolis: Lerner Classroom, 2007.
This is a brief but good outline of Ford's career. His father was an immigrant from Ireland.

Who Are You?
Writing Your Autobiography

Assignment

1. Use the following outline as a cluster to help you create an autobiography of your life. Describe your life up to now, your present life, and the future you hope to have.

2. Describe yourself in detail so that a classmate will easily recognize you.

3. Write your final draft in paragraph form.

First Paragraph: Your Past Life

Birth (time, place, circumstances): _____

_____

Family (people and pets): _____

_____

_____

_____

Grade school experiences (special teachers, joyful events, successes): _____

_____

_____

Second Paragraph: Your Present Life

Your physical looks (height, hair color, etc.): _____

_____

_____

Favorite school subjects: _____

Least favorite subjects: _____

Special friends (who they are and what you do together): _____

_____

_____

Who Are You?
Writing Your Autobiography *(cont.)*

Second Paragraph: Your Present Life *(cont.)*

Favorite sports and hobbies: _____

Personal interests in popular culture (music, bands, movies, etc.): _____

_____

Personal worries and concerns about family, friends, the world, and yourself: _____

_____

_____

Third Paragraph: Looking to the Future

Personal strengths (your abilities and character): _____

Educational goals (college and beyond): _____

Career goals (what you want to do with your life and why): _____

Personal goals (family and life choices): _____

Your Legacy

What special thing would you like to be remembered for doing—as a parent, public servant, or member of the community?

_____

_____

_____

Future Memories

What do you think you will remember about your life so far, especially about your childhood and school experiences?

_____

_____

_____

Discovering Your Immigrant Heritage

All Americans are descended from people who immigrated to America in the last 400 years or from American Indians. You can discover your personal immigrant heritage by doing this activity.

Assignment

1. Contact the oldest living relative you can find on the maternal (mother's) side of your family and the oldest relative you can find on the paternal (father's) side of your family.

    a. This person might be a grandparent or great-grandparent, an aunt, uncle, or cousin. In some cases, it might be your parents themselves. This could be because there are no older living relatives or your parents are the only source of information.

    b. If possible, meet in person or use the telephone to communicate with your relative. Or if he or she prefers, send e-mail or letters.

2. Ask if anyone in your family has any saved records, such as birth information, legal documents, pictures, or letters dating from the time of your family's immigration to this country.

3. Use the format below to organize the facts you learn.

4. If your family has been here so long that no relatives can be asked and no records exist, interview a neighbor who has a more recent history of immigration.

Maternal (Mother's) Family

Time period or years when the family came to America

_____

Reasons for immigrating to the United States

_____

_____

Who came (individual, parents, entire family)?

_____

_____

Where did the family enter the U.S.?

_____

_____

What dangers did they encounter from the trip?

_____

_____

How were they treated when they first arrived? (Were they welcomed, shunned, ignored, or mistreated when they arrived?)

_____

_____

Discovering Your Immigrant Heritage *(cont.)*

Maternal (Mother's) Family *(cont.)*

What challenges did they face in school?

_____

_____

How long have they lived in the United States?

_____

Where did your family live when they first arrived in the United States? (Did they move to different states or cities? Why?)

_____

_____

What work did they do to earn a living?

_____

_____

Paternal (Father's) Family

Time period or years when the family came to America

_____

Reasons for immigrating to the United States

_____

_____

Who came (individual, parents, entire family)?

_____

_____

Where did the family enter the U.S.?

_____

_____

What dangers did they encounter from the trip?

_____

_____

How were they treated when they first arrived? (Were they welcomed, shunned, ignored, or mistreated when they arrived?)

_____

_____

Discovering Your Immigrant Heritage *(cont.)*

Paternal (Father's) Family *(cont.)*

What challenges did they face in school?

_____

_____

How long have they lived in the United States?

_____

Where did your family live when they first arrived in the United States? (Did they move to different states or cities? Why?)

_____

_____

What work did they do to earn a living?

_____

_____

Evaluating the Experience

Describe the similarities and differences in the two families' experiences.

_____

_____

Describe your feelings about their efforts and experiences as immigrants.

_____

_____

_____

Cultural Inheritance

What cultural experiences have the families retained from their native lands? Respond to each given subject on the lines below.

Food (meals and desserts from the native countries)

_____

_____

Holiday Customs (particularly during the winter)

_____

_____

Clothes or Styles (influenced by the native countries)

_____

_____

John Muir and National Parks

One of the greatest public services by an immigrant was promoting a remarkable idea, the belief that some land should be preserved forever for all people to enjoy. John Muir believed some land should be left in its natural state, without logging and mining and with the wild animals protected. Muir was famous for exploring the first land granted by the federal government in the Yosemite Valley in California.

As he explored Yosemite, glaciers in Alaska, and other wild places, John Muir's writings on conservation began to influence important leaders and public opinion. His camping trip with President Theodore Roosevelt encouraged Roosevelt to support the idea, as well. Muir also founded the Sierra Club, which is dedicated to wildlife preservation.

The first national park to be established in the United States and, in fact, in the entire world was Yellowstone in 1872. It took a great deal of effort to convince Americans of the value of these parks, but by 1916, there were eleven parks and eighteen national monuments.

Assignment

Research each of the national parks listed on this page, as well as pages 87 and 88. Use the Internet, encyclopedias, almanacs, or books to help you. Find the information specified for each national park.

Yellowstone

Year it became a national park: _____

State(s) where it is located: _____

Size (acres): _____

Special features (land or water): _____

Special wildlife species (two): _____

Interesting fact(s): _____

Acadia

Year it became a national park: _____

State(s) where it is located: _____

Size (acres): _____

Special features (land or water): _____

Special wildlife species (two): _____

Interesting fact(s): _____

John Muir and National Parks *(cont.)*

Yosemite

Year it became a national park: _____

State(s) where it is located: _____

Size (acres): _____

Special features (land or water): _____

Special wildlife species (two): _____

Interesting fact(s): _____

Zion

Year it became a national park: _____

State(s) where it is located: _____

Size (acres): _____

Special features (land or water): _____

Special wildlife species (two): _____

Interesting fact(s): _____

Grand Canyon

Year it became a national park: _____

State(s) where it is located: _____

Size (acres): _____

Special features (land or water): _____

Special wildlife species (two): _____

Interesting fact(s): _____

Great Smoky Mountains

Year it became a national park: _____

State(s) where it is located: _____

Size (acres): _____

Special features (land or water): _____

Special wildlife species (two): _____

Interesting fact(s): _____

John Muir and National Parks *(cont.)*

Rocky Mountain

Year it became a national park: _____

State(s) where it is located: _____

Size (acres): _____

Special features (land or water): _____

Special wildlife species (two): _____

Interesting fact(s): _____

Mammoth Cave

Year it became a national park: _____

State(s) where it is located: _____

Size (acres): _____

Special features (land or water): _____

Special wildlife species (two): _____

Interesting fact(s): _____

Everglades

Year it became a national park: _____

State(s) where it is located: _____

Size (acres): _____

Special features (land or water): _____

Special wildlife species (two): _____

Interesting fact(s): _____

Evaluating Your Information

Which national park would you like to visit? Why? _____

_____

_____

Which national park is closest to where you live? Have you been there? _____

_____

John Muir and National Parks *(cont.)*

Assignment

1. Locate each of the national parks mentioned on pages 86–88 on the United States map below. Label each park on the appropriate state.

2. Use almanacs, encyclopedias, books, or the Internet to find and label ten more national parks on the appropriate states.

Celebrate Immigrant History Day

Set aside one day to be devoted to activities related to your study of American immigrants. If possible, celebrate with two or three classes at the same grade level. This allows you to share some of the group tasks and provides a special experience for the entire grade level.

Costumes

Encourage each of your students to come dressed in a costume related to the immigrant or American Indian culture they studied on pages 83 to 85. Parents may have some clothes, or they can visit thrift stores or sewing craft stores for materials.

Parent Help

Encourage as many parents or older siblings as you can to come for all or part of the day to enjoy the proceedings and to help set up and monitor the activities. This is truly a day to involve the family in the educational process. It helps to survey parents for any special talents, interests, or hobbies that would be a match for specific centers.

Doing Centers

- The centers you set up should relate in some way to the history of American immigrants.
- Centers should involve the children engaging in an activity and often making something they can take or put on display.
- The class should be divided into groups with about six or seven students in each group.
- Each center should take about twenty minutes. Students then rotate to the next activity.
- The following suggestions will get you started. Add any other activities to areas in which you have special expertise.

Sketching Immigrant Pictures

Each student could create a pencil sketch of one immigrant child or adult found in a resource book, a home diary, or online. You will need to have pictures and books available for the students to copy. You might also have your students who are in costume serve as models for the artists. You will need 9 x 12-inch pieces of white drawing or construction paper and dark lead pencils, colored pencils, or colored markers.

Quiz Show

Have students write questions (with answers) to be asked to individual students or teams in a quiz show format, like *Jeopardy*. The questions could be prepared ahead of time and given to a parent master of ceremonies.

Dancing

A simple ethnic dance could be learned or practiced in the time allotted for each center. At least one parent volunteer or teenager would be needed as a teacher.

Celebrate Immigrant History Day *(cont.)*

Clay Figures or Busts

In this center, students can use modeling clay or rectangular blocks of inexpensive sculpting clay to make figures or busts of some of the immigrants they studied. A twenty-five pound bag of inexpensive sculpting clay can be sliced into eighteen or more rectangular blocks of clay with a piece of fishing line. Use toothpicks to carve the features. Have paper towels available for cleanup.

Readers' Theater

The readers' theater center involves practicing with a script for a readers' theater presentation. The script could be the one in this book or one that children have written. Children at this center could also collaboratively write and perform a script.

Getting Around

Transportation is an important part of life in any era. Students could use this center to recreate one method of transportation used by immigrants. Steamships with steerage compartments would be excellent. Use small boxes, straws, craft sticks, modeling clay, and other materials to create any appropriate methods of transportation.

Poetry Center

This center would have "The New Colossus" on page 70 and other narrative poems in duplicate copies. Teams of students could present a poem together or as a group. Parents and other students would be the audience.

Read a Book

Students sometimes appreciate a quiet reading center as an activity break. Books by popular children's authors or short, easy stories would allow children a quiet period between more active centers.

Build the Statue of Liberty

Groups of students can use the pages in this book to build the Statue of Liberty (pages 68–70). They might also rebuild Ellis Island. This center could have poster board, construction paper, craft sticks, paint, and other craft items.

Learn a Game

Set up a center with some children's games from immigrant cultures or games learned in America. These would include baseball (the most popular game from the 1860s well into the twentieth century), soccer, races, and tag.

Eat Heartily

If you have parent volunteers, plan a potluck luncheon with an immigrant theme and foods from many lands and cultures. Parents and students could make the decorations together at one of the centers.

| 1600 | 1650 | 1700 | 1750 | 1800 | 1850 | 1900 | 1950 | 2000 |

Annotated Bibliography

History

Behnke, Alison. *Mexicans in America.* Minneapolis: Lerner, 2004.
  This is an excellent overview of Mexican immigration in the past and present.

Fisher, Leonard Everett. *Ellis Island: Gateway to the New World.* New York: Holiday House, 1986.
  This is a simple and photographed account of immigration through Ellis Island as experienced by immigrants themselves.

Flanagan, Alice K. *Angel Island.* Washington, DC: Compass Point, 2006.
  This is an easy-to-use story of the Chinese immigration through Angel Island to America.

Granfield, Linda. *97 Orchard Street, New York: Stories of Immigrant Life.* New York: Tundra Books, 2001.
  This includes pictures and short accounts of immigrant families who lived in one New York tenement over several decades.

Meltzer, Milton. *Bound for America: The Story of the European Immigrants.* New York: Benchmark, 2001.
  This is an interesting and complete account of the European migration to the United States from the 1820s to the 1920s.

Sandler, Martin W. *Immigrants: A Library of Congress Book.* New York: HarperCollins, 1995.
  This is an exceptional overview of immigration since 1800 with many historical photographs and easy-to-read text.

———. *Island of Hope: The Story of Ellis Island and the Journey to America.* New York: Scholastic, 2004.
  This is a superior history of Ellis Island with vignettes about and experiences of many of its immigrants.

Memoirs

Bierman, Carol. *Journey to Ellis Island.* New York: Hyperion, 1998.
  This is an illustrated true story of a Russian family's voyage to America and their Ellis Island experiences.

Wong, Li Keng. *Good Fortune: My Journey to Gold Mountain.* Atlanta: Peachtree, 2006.
  This is the true story of a Chinese girl and her family as they travel from a small village in China to America through Angel Island to a new life in Oakland's Chinatown.

Short Stories

Yee, Paul. *Tales from Gold Mountain: Stories of the Chinese in the New World.* New York: Macmillan, 1989.
  This is a collection of eight fascinating short stories about Chinese immigrants in the American West.

Novels

Napoli, Donna Jo. *The King of Mulberry Street.* New York: Random House, 2005.
  This is a high-energy novel of a nine-year-old Jewish Italian boy who stows away on a ship to America and survives on the tough streets of New York.

Tal, Eve. *Double Crossing.* El Paso: Cinco Puntos Press, 2005.
  This is a well-written, detailed novel of an eleven-year-old Jewish girl's journey with her father from Russia to Ellis Island in 1905.

Yep, Laurence and Kathleen Yep. *The Dragon's Child: A Story of Angel Island.* New York: HarperCollins, 2008.
  Based on conversations between Laurence Yep and his father, this novel tells the story of a boy's trip across the Pacific and his experiences on Angel Island.

Novels Used in This Book

Auch, Mary Jane. *Ashes of Roses.* New York: Holt, 2002.

Hesse, Karen. *Letters from Rifka.* New York: Holt, 1992.

Lasky, Kathryn. *Hope in My Heart: Sofia's Immigrant Diary.* New York: Scholastic, 2003.

Ryan, Pam Muñoz. *Esperanza Rising.* New York: Scholastic, 2000.

Glossary

alien—a person from another country

apprentice—a person who learns a skill from a craftsman

assimilate—to become a part of the larger culture and nation

citizen—a person living in a country with full rights, including the right to vote

competition—rivalry with other companies or workers in business

convict—a criminal who has been found guilty

debtor—a person who owes money

deport—to send someone back to their own country legally

deportee—a person legally sent away from a country

emigrant—a person leaving a country

epidemic—rapid spread of a disease to many people

exclusion—a policy of keeping out certain people because of national origin, race, or religion

famine—an extreme shortage of food

homeland—the native land of a person

illegal alien—a person who enters a country without legal permission

immigrant—a person entering a country

immigration—the movement of people from one country to another

indentured servant—a person who sold his services or the services of his family for about seven years to get to America

melting pot—a term suggesting that immigrants from many countries have formed one culture or country

passport—a form allowing legal entry into a country

persecution—injury or cruelty inflicted for reasons of race, religion, or national origin

pogrom—government-approved massacres of people for religious or political reasons

port of entry—a port where immigrants arrived in America

poverty—a condition where people lack food or any resources

propaganda—ideas that are misleading or false

quarantine—separating people with a contagious disease from others

refugee—a person displaced from his home by war, famine, or revolution

steerage class—travel on ships below decks in dirty, crowded conditions

strike—a refusal to work by employees in order to get better pay or working conditions

tenements—crowded apartments occupying large parts of cities

trachoma—a contagious eye disease

transatlantic—crossing the Atlantic Ocean

transcontinental—across a continent

undocumented alien—(see *illegal alien*)

unskilled labor—people without education or specialized training

vermin—unwanted mice, rats, and insects

Answer Key

Page 34
1. b
2. c
3. d
4. d
5. d
6. c
7. a
8. d
9. a
10. d

Page 35
1. b
2. d
3. d
4. b
5. a
6. c
7. d
8. a
9. b
10. d

Page 36
1. d
2. b
3. d
4. a
5. d
6. b
7. c
8. d
9. b
10. c

Page 37
1. b
2. c
3. c
4. c
5. a
6. d
7. d
8. d
9. d
10. a

Page 38
1. b
2. b
3. a
4. c
5. d
6. b
7. c
8. d
9. d
10. d

Page 39
1. a
2. d
3. a
4. b
5. a
6. d
7. c
8. b
9. d
10. d

Page 40
1. c
2. a
3. c
4. c
5. b
6. a
7. b
8. d
9. a
10. a

Page 41
1. c
2. b
3. b
4. c
5. b
6. c
7. c
8. b
9. b
10. b

Page 45
1. persecution
2. indentured servant
3. port of entry
4. melting pot
5. famine
6. debtor
7. exclusion
8. competition
9. convict
10. poverty
11. apprentice
12. epidemic
13. assimilate
14. immigration
15. emigrant

Page 46

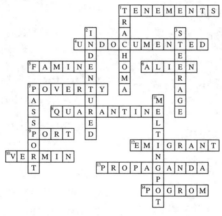

Page 47
2. Greek; common people
3. French; rude person or child
4. Arabic; a religious command
5. French; a done deal
6. French; a person who likes expensive food
7. Tagalog; rural area
8. Spanish; grocery store
9. Russian; intellectual group
10. Japanese; Japanese animation
11. Italian; outdoors
12. French; compared with
13. Yiddish or German; an honorable person
14. Italian or Latin; expert
15. German; an inferior substitute
16. French; full power to act
17. French; a social mistake

18. French; newly rich
19. French; joy of living
20. Spanish; a confrontation

Page 48
1. to have a wild time
2. to get away from
3. in deep trouble
4. to pay a lot
5. unsatisfactory or defective
6. teasing me
7. talking nonsense or bragging
8. exhausted or finished
9. to tackle the problem directly
10. was suspicious

Page 55
Comprehension Questions
Answers will vary but may be similar to:
1. They leave to get away from the uncles.
2. She won't let the poor child touch her doll.
3. Esperanza's mom gets Valley Fever, but she recovers.
4. He takes the money orders to bring their grandmother to California, which is what the money was being saved for.
5. She has to avoid the uncles. She hides in a convent.
6. She gives the doll to Isabel.

Discussion Starters
Answers will vary but may be similar to:
1. Isabel doesn't win because she is Mexican.
2. The uncles are probably responsible for the father's murder, although they may have hired someone to do it.
3. The immigrants face discrimination in school, public facilities (the pool), and in getting good jobs.
4. The passage of time is counted by the produce being harvested—melons, asparagus, etc.

Answer Key *(cont.)*

Page 55 *(cont.)*

5. Hortensia and her family are clearly devoted to Esperanza's mother and the family and were probably well treated by Esperanza's father.
6. Esperanza and her mother can't afford the risk of forcible deportation back to Mexico.
7. Answers will vary.
8. Answers will vary.

Page 56
Discussion Starters
Answers will vary but may be similar to:

1. They flee to protect their boys from being forced into the Russian army.
2. They have some wealth and are getting along fairly well.
3. It is a gift from Tovah, and she loves the poetry.
4. They are chased by guards, they get ill with typhus, some belongings are stolen, and Rifka can't go to America because of ringworm.
5. The boys would be forced into the Russian army, and the family would have no way to live and could be punished by the Russians for trying to leave.
6. She reads well, enjoys poetry, and gets along well with people.
7. She probably got it from the scalp of the Polish girl on the train.
8. They help her become more open to and understanding of people and life. She matures through her experiences.
9. She helps Ilya understand English, gets him to eat, and is kind and understanding with the detainees.

10. Answers will vary.
11. She is talkative and assertive.
12. They love each other, but they like to argue. Rifka is envious of him at times.

Page 57
Discussion Starters
Answers will vary but may be similar to:

1. Answers will vary.
2. They are locked in to keep them from stealing things or wasting time away from the machines.
3. Answers will vary.
4. She learns to stand up for herself, to trust very few people, and to adjust to American ways.
5. She thinks she's better than Rose's family, and she doesn't want Patrick to spend money on or time with them.
6. Irish, Jewish, Russian, Polish and other cultures are encountered.

Page 58
Comprehension Questions

1. Gabriella
2. She has trachoma.
3. Rafi is a boy in quarantine who knows all the secrets of the island.
4. She helps Mr. Joe, Maureen, Coco, and others.
5. Ireland
6. Father Finnegan, Nancy, and Rafi help in different ways.

Discussion Starters
Answers will vary but may be similar to:

1. He shows her how things really work at Ellis Island.
2. She doesn't speak English very well, and the culture is different from her native land of Italy.
3. She is determined, brave, and concerned about others.
4. They think she is mentally unbalanced and has an eye

disease because her eye is swollen.
5. They are mistreated by people who can get away with it and don't care about the immigrants.
6. Answers will vary.
7. Answers will vary.
8. Answers will vary.

Page 69

153 cm	2 cm
56 cm	7 cm
8 cm	12 cm
4 cm	1 cm
5 cm	45 cm
2 cm	33 cm
21 cm	

Page 74

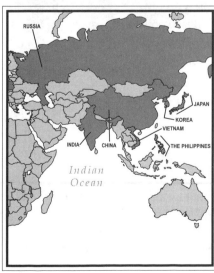

Answer Key *(cont.)*

Page 75
1. 4,650,000
2. 1,800,000
3. 3,000,000
4. 3,300,000
5. 3,900,000
6. 3,000,000
7. 4,800,000
8. 3,600,000
9. 900,000
10. 300,000

Page 76
1. 105 days
2. 33.3% or 33%
3. 6.6% or 7%
4. 2,740
5. more than 500,000
   100,000
6. 82
7. 75%
8. 98.8% or 99%

Page 77
Germany	43,935,000
Africa	36,360,000
Ireland	30,300,000
England	24,240,000
Mexico	20,907,000
Italy	15,756,000
Poland	9,090,000
France	8,181,000
Scotland	4,848,000
Holland	4,545,000
American Indian	3,030,000
Native Hawaiian/ Pacific Islander	606,000
Asian	13,332,000
Black	38,784,000
Hispanic/Latino	45,753,000
White (not Hispanic)	242,703,000
Foreign-born	36,663,000
Under twenty-one years of age	74,235,000
Over sixty-five years of age	38,178,000
Over eighty-five years of age	5,454,000

Pages 86–88

Yellowstone
Year: 1872
States: Wyoming, Montana, and Idaho
Size: 2.2 million acres
Features: 10,000 geysers/ hot springs
Wildlife species: grizzly bear, bison, moose
Fact: Mudpots bubble at earth's surface.

Acadia
Year: 1919 (but it wasn't called Acadia until 1929)
State: Maine
Size: 47,000 acres
Features: part on the mainland and part on an island
Wildlife species: beaver, peregrine falcon, salamander
Fact: Cadillac Mountain in the park is the highest point on the East coast.

Yosemite
Year: 1890
State: California
Size: 747,956 acres
Features: highest waterfall in nation
Wildlife species: black bear, spotted owl, bobcat
Fact: The name "Yosemite" is derived from an American Indian tribal name meaning grizzly bear.

Zion
Year: 1919
State: Utah
Size: 148,016 acres
Features: unusual shapes and landforms, such as a horsehead in West Temple; Great White Throne monolith
Wildlife species: bighorn sheep, mule deer, mountain lion
Fact: Weeping Rock Cliff provides an oasis in the desert environment.

Grand Canyon
Year: 1919
State: Arizona
Size: 1,217,403 acres
Features: Colorado River divides park into North Rim and South Rim
Wildlife species: California condors, porcupines, bats
Fact: The canyon is more than 277 miles long, more than a mile deep, and 18 miles wide in some places.

Great Smoky Mountains
Year: 1934
States: North Carolina and Tennessee
Size: 522,052 acres
Features: The Appalachian Trail runs through this park.
Wildlife species: black bears, red-tailed hawks, and eight species of turtles
Fact: It is the most frequently visited national park.

Rocky Mountain
Year: 1915
State: Colorado
Size: 265,770 acres
Features: Trail Ridge (highest road in any U.S. National Park at 12,183')
Wildlife species: beaver, bighorn sheep, three-toed woodpecker
Fact: The Continental Divide runs along the crest of the mountains.

Mammoth Cave
Year: 1941
State: Kentucky
Size: 52,830 acres
Features: 365 miles of explored caves; River Styx (underground river) is over 300 feet below surface.
Wildlife species: bats, cave shrimp, wild turkeys
Facts: Frozen Niagara looks like a giant white waterfall. It's the world's longest (known) cave.

Everglades
Year: 1947 (authorized in 1934)
State: Florida
Size: 1,509,000 acres
Features: Huge area of wetlands; swamps; seas of wet grasslands
Wildlife species: alligators, manatees, green (sea) turtles
Fact: This is the only place in the world where alligators and crocodiles coexist.